I Was a Flakey Preacher

I WAS A FLAKEY PREACHER

Ted Brooks

Belleville, Ontario, Canada

I Was a Flakey Preacher
Copyright © 1999, Ted Brooks

All Rights Reserved. No part of this publication may be reproduced, stored in a retrieval system or transmitted in any form or by any means – electronic, mechanical, photocopy, recording or any other – except for brief quotations in printed reviews, without the prior permission of the author.

All Scripture quotations unless otherwise indicated are the New King James Version of the Bible (Copyright © 1979, 1980, 1982 Thomas Nelson Inc.)

Author's emphases are in italics or in parentheses embedded into the Bible text.

ISBN: 1-894169-79-4

**For more information or
to order additional copies, please contact:**

Testing the Spirits
9739-99 Street
Westlock, Alberta, Canada
T7P 1Y5

www.testingthespirits.com

Printed in Canada
by
Guardian BOOKS

◆ Table of Contents

Chapter One
I Was a Flake and Didn't Know It 7

Chapter Two
Jesus Came in the Flesh 27

Chapter Three
Test the Spirits 36

Chapter Four
Signs and Wonders 53

Chapter Five
The Devil Wants Zion 60

Chapter Six
Beware the False Prophet 63

Chapter Seven
Submission to Leadership 75

Chapter Eight
New Doctrines and Movements 80

Chapter Nine
Familiar Spirits Exposed 114

Chapter Ten
Divination. 120

Chapter Eleven
Spirits of the Dead 126

Chapter Twelve
Balaam 130

Chapter Thirteen
Jannes and Jambres. 138

Chapter Fourteen
Cleansing the Spots and Wrinkles 141

◆ Chapter One

I WAS A FLAKE AND DIDN'T KNOW IT

Flake: *noun, slang*, 1. An eccentric person; an oddball. 2. A wacky or dizzy person. i.e.: the wacky professor. 3. A nut; someone who is spinny; dizzy; strange.

Although this word is slang, it is used extensively throughout Christian circles to describe Christians, preachers, and zealous leaders who do not remain established in solid doctrine. In many cases, flakes are talented preachers who simply have ventured beyond common biblical conduct.

In our Christian culture, this includes eccentric preachers who do wild, enthusiastic things which appear spiritual to the undiscerning – but under closer examination, we discover that they trespass biblical standards.

Flakey preachers are filled with prophetic babbling, empty headed foolishness, and deep spiritual speculation.

A flakey preacher is someone who cannot back up his beliefs and actions with solid biblical teaching. He gets his ideas from somewhere out there in the spirit realm: "The Spirit of the Lord just showed me...." A flakey preacher is also someone who lacks scriptural substance.

Flakes are often people whose doctrines contain only a sliver of truth while covered over with an abundance of fluff.

In more recent years, I have used "Flake" as a title to describe false prophets who use great swelling words of emptiness (2 Peter 2:18).

Flakes, fruits, and nuts are "granola bar" Christians because they stick together. I have joked about this many times, in the past, but I did not realize that it actually applied to me.

I Was One of Them

Along with many others, I was a flakey preacher walking on thin doctrinal ice. I was a dangerous leader to follow because I would lead people into spiritual experiences which had little scriptural support.

It is not that I did not have any truth: it is just that I misused it. I was a preacher who appeared to have spiritual knowledge, but when I finally came to my senses I realized that I used only a bit of truth. The Gospel I dished out was only a small portion of what it was supposed to be.

So why did people listen to me? The reason was very simple: I appeared to be as friendly and talented as any other Charismatic preacher – or so I thought. My deception was neatly hidden under several layers of enthusiasm. It was hard to stop and analyze what was going on because of the momentum of my zeal. I did everything with my whole heart and didn't have time to doubt or to discern my doctrines.

Was I just one of the few who was deceived? No, I don't think so. Flakey leaders are more common among us than we would like to admit. As I repented of my foolishness I was able to see that many leaders in the Church were standing on thin doctrinal ice. It dawned on me that flakiness was not a small problem in the Church.

Chapter One

WE WERE ALL IN THE SAME FOG

I wasn't always flakey. There was a time in my life when I was at least beginning to understand the importance of the New Testament revelation of Christ. The foundation of Christ was an important doctrine which I was starting to understand; but at the same time, I found that the revelation of Christ alienated me somewhat from my Charismatic peers. A strong desire to "belong" overruled biblical understanding. Therefore, in the name of unity and getting along with my brothers, I began to mix extra-biblical doctrines into my thinking. This allowed me to fit in with my preacher friends for a period of time. However, as time passed, I continued to search my own heart and began to compare the solid revelation of Christ with my favorite Charismatic teachings. I started to scrutinize my own camp's beliefs. This was where an inevitable conflict arose.

I WAS SUSPICIOUS

Several years ago, I was meditating upon this conflict and I was trying to settle several issues. I was attempting to cooperate and work with several leaders in our church fellowship, as well as with those of other churches in our community. But, at the same time, I was suspicious of the genuineness of some of the wild, miraculous claims among leaders and peers around me. In my heart, I knew there was something wrong with several of the spiritual manifestations we were experiencing. And since I had very little biblical proof, I couldn't quite put my finger on what it was. When I finally searched the scriptures, I could find little scriptural proof for what we as leaders claimed as "from God." In fact, a few of our associates claimed to be involved in frequent, fantastic spiritual experiences which were way beyond anything I was experiencing. I couldn't find anything in the Bible to substantiate these strange claims.

Sadly though, we did not challenge any of the manifestations in each other at the time because we had been trained to "walk in love" and to "look for the best in people." It wasn't proper to challenge a "brother" regarding doctrine, so we just kept on going into more deception. We were the blind leading the blind, ignoring the issues, unaware that we were "Word poor" and all the while thinking we were rich in revelation.

About that time, I began to have an intense desire to study the concept of "false" in the Bible. I didn't realize it at the time, but the biblical insight I was about to learn was destined to change my perception of the Christian life and my entire outlook on the ministry. Eventually, this scriptural search set me free from many false concepts I held as a Charismatic Christian. It answered many of the nagging questions with which I struggled.

THE BIBLE HELPED ME REALIZE I WAS A FLAKE

As I researched "false," I began to suspect that I was just as flakey as the leaders with whom I was sharing leadership! The fist of accusation always has one finger pointing at the accused and three more pointing back to its owner. I realized we were all in the same fog.

As I studied, I found answers to many questions like:

1. How could we as Christians and leaders appear so accurate in spiritual information when yielding to wrong spirits?

2. How was it possible for false teachers to deceive those of us who had been Christians for a long time or those of us who were experienced leaders?

3. Why did Jesus warn His disciples and us so often about deception in the last days?

Chapter One

I wanted to clarify this point: by studying "false," I am not talking about the cults. There are many large Christian ministries which specialize in exposing cult activity and doctrine. Sadly though, this can have a weakening effect on those who claim to be leaders in discernment. They risk becoming specialists in wrong doctrine while remaining uneducated in true Bible doctrine. The danger is they can appear to be knowledgeable, but their knowledge is not based on God's Word.

IT IS LIKE SPOTTING COUNTERFEIT CURRENCY

Investigating the many facets of counterfeit money is only effective when combined with adequate training in handling real currency. In fact, it is well known in the banking industry, that the best person to spot a counterfeit bill is the one who has handled an abundance of genuine bills. The same can be applied to the Church: the best defense against false doctrine is to be well educated in the doctrine of Christ. Analyzing cult doctrine will never have the same impact as reading the Word of God and seeing what it has to say about false teachings.

This is what happened in my life. The written Word of God was enough, by itself, to challenge the foolishness in my life. I was also convinced that the doctrine of Christ was more than adequate to correct and convince any person in false religion as well. The Word of God contained plenty of information and revelation concerning the false. The genuine revelation of Christ was the best place to find the wisdom and understanding needed to expose the wiles of the Devil.

The Word of God had much to reveal to me about false teachers, false apostles, false doctrine, and false prophets. This may sound like a negative subject to some, but this research was positive for me because it set me free from the things I could not see at the time.

THE PROBLEM WAS AN OLD ONE

I was raised in a Pentecostal church where we believed in miracles, visions, tongues, and the gift of prophecy. It was in my younger years, that I was exposed to all kinds of supposed spiritual manifestations and testimonies. I was literally spellbound as I watched people weave, shake, and fall in special prayer lines. And the testimonies were captivating to say the least. Anything from, "The Lord told me..." to visions of demons in the rafters and devils shouting accusations against their lifestyles. Then add to that the stories of past revivals. It became obvious to me very early why we were called "Holy Rollers."

After sharing this story with a preacher friend of mine, he told me, "Ted, you didn't have a chance." He was reminding me that it was inevitable for me to become a flake because error was all around me.

"HUBBA, HUBBA, HUBBA"

In my home church there was one man in particular who "prophesied" in almost every meeting. He seemed to be the typical "yielded vessel," but none among us were strong enough to challenge him when he "yielded" to wrong spirits. His prophecies were "silly and empty," but – so were we. That is why we went along with it. There wasn't enough Word in us to know any better. He would always start out the same way: "Hubba hubba hubba, hubba hubba hubba," and then he would interpret with a profound statement like: "Christmas is of the Devil," or "Snowmobiles are evil."

However, we didn't have enough understanding of the Word of God to be able to judge what was false and what was true, so

Chapter One

we were easily led astray to think that this kind of thing was of God. Add to this the many testimonies that were encouraged by the pastor. We heard anything from, "Devils in the rafters," to "The Lord told me to go to the store." The pastor seemed to allow this to carry on without even hinting to us that it could be questioned. It was spiritual activity like this that started me on the road to error. Mind you, now that I look back, I don't think the pastors had any authority to correct us, even if they did suspect that things were flakey. After all, the pastors were hired and fired by the people in the church. How could the pastors then stand against false prophecy under those conditions? Their jobs were on the line. So I am sure it was easier for them to just allow the flakiness to continue unchecked.

While listening to me share some these issues a friend once asked me, "Well, didn't you *feel* that something was wrong?" Sure, I *felt* many things, but discernment is not based on a feeling. True discernment only comes from the living Word of God. In fact, thinking that discernment was based on feelings led me ever deeper into error.

The Word of God had to come alive in my heart first. Then, and only then, was I able to truly discern.

Praying for Spooky Buildings

I once worked among leaders in a Charismatic church where we frequently boasted to each other of our incredible experiences in the Spirit. Some leaders claimed to have a remarkable supernatural ability to go into a house and pray in every room until a spiritual message came to them. The "spirit" would then reveal the important history of the home to them. Whether this information was accurate or not was not known to us nor could it be proven or disproven. Nevertheless, they would claim that they suddenly knew every negative, spiritually significant, or important occasion that ever happened in that house. Then they would do spiritual warfare over the building.

As Christians, we didn't know this kind of practice was unbiblical. We were unknowingly yielding to flesh and wrong spirits. Our words sounded mystical and spiritual, which entertained the undiscerning; but we were sadly lacking the fullness of the Gospel of Jesus Christ. We were experiencing some amazing spiritual sensations which were often very overwhelming indeed; but, in most cases, they were not the work of the Holy Spirit.

SPIRITUAL WARFARE

Has the Church fallen for this kind of thing? Yes it has! Instead of *preaching* the Lordship of Christ to individuals, we are trying to *pray* the Lordship of Christ over their environments through spiritual warfare. If we aren't praying, then we are picketing, protesting, and trying in vain to make unrighteous leaders bow to righteous demands.

We have been commissioned by Jesus to preach the Gospel to people. We have not been commissioned to pray for spooky buildings, to be involved in political activism, or demand the moral transformation of our unrighteous nations.

Now, what does this have to do with spooky buildings? Well, instead of preaching the Gospel to the people who lived in the old house, my associates were trying in vain to change their spiritual environment.

The Church does the same thing. Instead of preaching the Gospel to individuals in our nation, we are desperately trying, through spiritual warfare, to change the spiritual environment of the nation first. In all this, the Devil is very active because this kind of spiritual warfare bypasses the Gospel of Christ.

Chapter One

IT IS CLOUDY IN HERE

Throughout the following years, we continued to experience many visions and supernatural sensations. As I look back, I realize that they were nothing more than vain, meaningless images, and empty-headed illusions of flowers and clouds, black spheres in our hands, and demons in the attic. The fruit of the Gospel and knowing Christ was missing or at least lacking in our doctrines and our lifestyles. We were dancing with deception; not entirely mind you, but just enough to seduce us and keep us captivated and enticed with wrong doctrines and wrong actions.

Of course, some of our leaders were better at "yielding" than others. And had we been better at discerning, their preaching alone would often have revealed much. At times, their messages appeared to be very mystical. You must keep in mind that this was a favorable thing in our camp. We were greatly impressed when leaders' messages were "spooky, unclear, and cloudy," especially when the "spirit moved." I must admit to you, that at times there seemed to be a heavy feeling, an awesome atmosphere, and an intoxicating spiritual presence in many meetings – especially during a moving prophetic word or a special revelation. Without proper biblical knowledge, it was very hard to discern whether this was the presence of the Spirit of God or the presence of wrong spirits. We were taught that the presence of the Holy Spirit (or the anointing) was a heavy feeling; and since we were trained to discern by our feelings, we were easily led astray.

PUTTING MY DISCERNMENT TO THE TEST

For me, 1992-93 was a period of soul searching and learning more about the false. During that time, I had a good opportunity to put my new knowledge to the test. While visiting a preacher friend in his office, another man dropped by to say "hello." The man was a local farmer/trapper on his way to the city to witness on the streets. His unclean appearance bothered me at first, but I tried to overlook it. After all, God looks at the heart; we were trained to look for the best in people. If he was on his way to witness on the streets, well, surely a person who was zealous to preach was on the up and up. But as he began to share his testimony, I realized that his outward appearance was more than just an oversight. It also matched his inward "uncleanness" and "flakiness." He claimed he had experienced several angelic visitations on his trapline in the woods. This alerted me to something deeper, so I asked him to tell me more. As he continued, he made it sound like his salvation, his spiritual knowledge, and his experiences, all came via numerous angelic visitations.

Rolling Around in the Sea of Galilee

My Pentecostal preacher friend was not so alarmed with all this and seemed to politely accept this as normal spiritual activity. I pressed the man for more information in hopes that his foolishness would become obvious. I wanted my friend's eyes to be opened to what was going on. The trapper continued to tell story after incredible story. The last was astounding to say the least. He claimed that angels had picked him up and carried him halfway around the world to deposit him in the middle of the Sea of Galilee. He told us it was a thrill for him to roll around in its beautiful waters for quite some time, before the angels transported him back to his trapline.

I challenged the man to consider that perhaps the experience lacked scriptural backing and could very well have been an overactive imagination or even demonic activity. This made him very angry. By this time, my preacher friend looked nervous and I felt pressured to back down from my stand. After all, it wasn't my office, it was his. Although the stranger shouted accusations at me as he made his way to the door, I didn't crumble. I held my ground. My new biblical knowledge of the false was helping me discern what was biblical and what was flakey.

"Brother, I Have a Word for You"

As time went on, I continued to study the Bible, learning more and more about the false, getting stronger at confronting it, and learning how to tactfully expose flakey thinking. In our corporate gatherings, a new standard was being raised. Where we had previously allowed just about anyone to publicly prophesy in our meetings, we were beginning to discern the flakes. We were getting better at challenging unruly visitors, church hoppers, and those among us who wanted to steer the spiritual direction of our church.

In an ironic way, we ourselves were responsible for this trend. Our Charismatic church and others like it had become well known for being open to public comments from visitors. One Sunday morning, we subdued a visitor who kept shouting, "Brother, I have a word for you from the Lord." I did not allow him to prophesy to me and asked him to refrain from speaking out. But because he continued to be very aggressive and loud, I didn't wait until the end of the service to explain why. I corrected him from the pulpit, explained to the people my reasons, and then continued my preaching. Amazingly though, this did not deter him. He then attempted to give a "word" to one of our ushers who stopped him once again. This thrilled my heart because it showed me that there were others in our church who were getting stronger at confronting the flakes.

After the service, the stranger came up to me and asked me to agree with him in prayer for something. He told me he wanted to pray for the breakup of his daughter's marriage. I responded, "I'm sorry, but I don't do Charismatic witchcraft." He just smiled and said, "That's a very interesting way of putting it."

It Was Hard to Confront Our Own Identity

During this time, confrontation was hard for me: as I was challenging these manifestations, I was actually challenging my own church's spiritual style. This style was hard to confront because it was part of my identity as a Charismatic preacher and it was based on many years of flakey tradition. (I think the struggle would be the same for anyone who is still involved in those circles.)

None of us are immune to the common deceptions of our peers and nothing shakes us more than the earthquake of our own traditions crumbling underneath our feet.

"From Thirty Degrees to Seventy"

Another man visited our church occasionally and his idea of spiritual warfare was to tie a rock music T-shirt to the bumper of his truck and drag it around town. At first, we thought this was a great idea and a bold witness for Jesus. But as we grew in biblical knowledge, we repented for respecting such foolishness.

The last time I saw him, he approached me in a restaurant, walked up to my table, and boldly proclaimed that he had seen a vision of God's judgment. He said, "I saw the judgment of God at thirty degrees increasing to seventy degrees." I asked him, "Where is that in the Bible?" He looked at me like I had lost my spiritual marbles. He walked away in disgust and hasn't spoken to me since.

A Great Cleansing

By confronting the flakiness that was a strong part of our church, I was learning something vital. The false was being cleansed out of our church in two scriptural ways. The first was in the hearts of those who would listen, repent, and change. The other was the departure of those who would not be corrected. Either way, we were thrilled with the results. Our church was getting stronger and we were being cleansed.

Overwhelming Experiences

For some people, it was hard for them to let go of their flakiness. False visions and experiences can seem very powerful and real. I know how strong they can be, because I yielded to these kinds of things on a regular basis.

There is no doubt that these sensations can be overwhelming; but if you are walking in the feelings of your flesh like I was, and not in the knowledge of the Word, you will not be able to discern the difference between "soul" and "spirit" and feelings will take over.

These experiences are very spiritual and real to those who are yielding to them. This is just my point; they seemed real to me because of the awesome power I thought I was experiencing, but the results were very harmful and deceptive.

A Great Prophetic Word

A vital part of our church life for many years has been a prayer/share time every weekday morning from seven o'clock to eight. A classic example of overpowering experiences happened to me on one of these morning sessions several years ago. As I approached the church, I was in anguish and frustration over the small church I pastored and the small town I lived in. The more I challenged the doctrines of our past, the more the church shrank in size. Fewer people were willing to stay and be challenged. I have to admit though, I did have a secret ambition which I thought was noble. There was a major city one hour away and I was thinking, "If only God would call me to the big city, all my problems would be over." That morning, I experienced something so powerful, so overwhelming, so "prophetic," that I was convinced, beyond a shadow of a doubt, that I was to move my entire ministry and every willing family to Edmonton, Alberta and start another church.

After sharing this with the congregation, we started travelling one day per week to hold meetings in the city. There was some degree of success, but as time went on, I realized in my own heart that the prophetic experience was false. During that time, I was still studying and learning about false prophecies in the Word. I shared my findings at the city meetings.

What I was preaching in Edmonton was exposing the false in others; but it was also convicting me and showing me where I went wrong. The very fact that the morning prayer experience was overwhelming was one indicator, but the other factor was, I was relying on feelings and circumstantial evidence to lead the church. The Word of God was being bypassed in this decision.

After several months, we practiced what we preached. We stopped having the meetings in the city, settled back into our own church, and again became content and satisfied in the wonderful things that God was showing us through His Word. It was a bit embarrassing to admit our mistake, but it was a good lesson for us all.

Later, it occurred to me that I could go and preach in Edmonton, or in any city for that matter, anytime there was opportunity, simply because the Word said, "Go." I did not have to be overwhelmed by some mysterious experience in order to be called by God. It was much more fulfilling to be motivated by God's Living Word.

SUBJECT TO THE PROPHET

Paul, the Apostle, taught how true spiritual gifts were subject to the prophet and how the true manifestations of the Spirit would not overpower a person who wanted to be a yielded vessel. Based on that teaching, I learned that experiences which cannot be controlled or held in check by ordinary people are usually not the work of the Holy Spirit.

"And the spirits of the prophets are subject to the prophets" (1 Corinthians 14:32).

The ultimate example of this would be Jesus because He was the firstborn of many brethren (Romans 8:29). He is the original pattern for all the children of God and the benchmark for true spiritual reality.

In His earthly ministry, Jesus did not overpower anyone with a manifestation that could not be stopped. Today the Holy Spirit is given to us to reveal the same anointing that He manifested through Jesus' earthly ministry. We must remember that He never overpowered a person with uncontrollable manifestations which they couldn't resist, and neither will He do it today. What the Holy Spirit anointed Jesus to do during His earthly ministry is our eternal benchmark.

THE "DIP AND POUR" PREACHER

After I grew in more knowledge and discernment, I was invited to a special meeting by a pastor whom I hadn't seen in many years. We had attended the same Pentecostal Bible College when we were younger. But both of us were also influenced strongly by the Word of Faith movement and I thought it would be good to renew an old acquaintance.

There was a guest speaker at this meeting of whom I had heard ten years previously. He was a Word of Faith preacher who had written a book about the Blood of Jesus more than a dozen years before. Based on that fact alone, I thought the meeting would be fairly solid.

As the meeting progressed, it became very evident to me that what the preacher may have had years ago, had all but vanished. He preached a very stirring message which entertained the undiscerning, but contained hardly a trace of the Gospel of Jesus Christ.

His sermon was a collection of emotional and spiritual experiences of yesteryear, which didn't seem too harmful at first; but, as the evening progressed, the sermon became amazing to say the least. Near the end of his message, he began sharing some of his spiritual dreams. These strange visions and experiences had the audience spellbound. In one of his visions, the man claimed he fell into a pool of liquid and was able to breathe under the surface. A famous man of God entered the dream (approval by association) and commanded the preacher to pick up an amethyst ladle to dip and pour the liquid out of the pool for others to experience.

The preacher began to tell this vision with great emotional emphasis, "Then... (the man of God) told me to dip and pour, (louder) dip and pour, (louder) dip and pour... (pause and soften for emphasis) and that is what we are going to experience tonight!" The audience cheered! He went on to say, "Every person in this room is going to come to the front of this church and I will lay my hands on you to experience this...."

I did not want the "this" he was trying to sell, so I took advantage of the shuffle to make my way to the exit. He didn't

Chapter One

realize that the thing he wanted us to experience was empty and foolish. But no one else seemed to be concerned. After all, more than two hundred people can't all be wrong – can they?

I Mustered the Courage to Expose It

It took me three months to muster enough courage to talk to the pastor who had invited me to the meeting. When I told him what I had discerned, my friend became very angry with me. It was at times like this that I wished I had never said anything.

I was like a blind man who had received his sight. I was amazed with what I could see. Foolishness I had formerly accepted without question, now became obvious to me. I began to challenge my peers with what I had found. But I wasn't prepared for the tremendous resistance that would come from them. I felt it would have been best not to say anything. Later on, I realized that it was nothing more than the fear of man which made me want to pull back. I became determined to grow in discernment, even if it meant losing my friends. I loved being able to see.

As discernment increased in my life, I realized that preachers overlook a lot of spiritual foolishness in their churches. It is not because they don't love the people; it is because they are afraid to confront. They don't question their own spiritual or denominational roots; therefore, they do not know how to judge for themselves.

How Long Does It Take?

What happened to the "dip and pour" preacher? How did this man become a cloud without content and a well without water? (2 Peter 2:17) When did the original Gospel of Jesus Christ fade from this man's preaching?

Based on my own experience, I am convinced it took many years for mysticism to replace the Word of God in this man's life and ministry; and it probably took a while to manifest in his public preaching.

It didn't happen overnight in my life either. It took several years to distract me from the little bit of truth I possessed.

Deception and emptiness are always progressive: they creep into a minister's life ever so slowly. It probably took ten years or more to cause the "dip and pour" preacher to turn to emptiness and spiritual foolishness.

The Devil is a cunning, slow-moving serpent. But if he gets a grip on your theology, he will slowly choke the life-giving Word out of you. He hates truth, and he will do anything within his power to steal the Word from you. This is the reason why Jesus told the Jews who believed on Him to *continue* in the Word.

"Then Jesus said to those Jews who believed Him, "If you *abide (continue)* in My word, you are My disciples indeed. And you shall know the truth, and the truth shall make you free" (John 8:31-32).

In order to be free from deception, and stay free, we must *continue* in the Word. We cannot afford to stop, especially in these days. We are called to be disciples of truth. We must continually grow in biblical doctrine and revelation. We should never think that we can bypass or go beyond the written Word.

The First Temptation

The Devil will try to tempt us to experience supernatural sensations or to walk in exclusive revelations which side-step the revealed and written will of God.

He did the same thing to Eve in the garden of Eden. The Devil asked her, "Has God said?" And he has been trying to

Chapter One

deceive man with the same trick ever since. He loves to malign the Word of God.

You may ask, "But, how does that apply to us?" This applies to us today as much as it applied to Eve. Paul writes to New Testament believers, "But I fear, lest somehow, as the serpent deceived Eve by his craftiness, so your minds may be corrupted from the *simplicity* that is in Christ" (2 Corinthians 11:3). That's right, the Gospel of Jesus Christ is simple! It is the will of God made clear and understandable. Jesus came to be the *one and only source* for salvation, healing, deliverance, and truth. God did not provide multiple paths to Himself. He only provided one. This is the simplicity of the Gospel. This seemingly narrow Gospel is the power of God and is more than sufficient for every one of us.

The Devil is still saying, "Are you sure God said that? Has God really spoken everything He wanted to say through His Word? Isn't there more to it? Surely God left out some details! Maybe He doesn't trust you with the whole truth! There may be some things He neglected to tell you!"

The Devil hasn't changed a bit. He still wants us to deviate from God's original plan. He wants us to think, "The Word of God is not enough. There is more revelation to be had beyond the living Word."

One of the Devil's most subtle weapons is to pretend to be the Holy Spirit. The Devil wants to be an alternate source of inspiration and illumination. He does this by disguising himself as an angel of light (2 Corinthians 11:14). His goal is to reveal knowledge which is beyond proper biblical revelation and credit it to the inspiration of the Holy Spirit.

The Devil suggested to Eve, "God knows that as soon as you eat the fruit of that tree you will know more than you do now. There is revelation in that fruit. Take a bite! God knows you will be just like Him if you eat it. As soon as you do, you will know more than you do now."

THE END RESULT IS ALWAYS THE SAME

It is interesting to note, after Adam and Eve tasted the fruit and their eyes were opened, all they saw was their own shame and nakedness. The promised revelation never came to pass.

The Devil's goal was to get Eve to venture beyond God's Word, which was given to her as a simple command. Satan made it sound like there was a wonderful reward waiting for her if she transgressed God's instructions.

We still have a simple Word to heed. It is the Gospel and revelation of Jesus Christ. The Devil is desperately trying to entice and convince us to transgress it. The truth is, the simple yet powerful Gospel of Jesus Christ is more than enough to set us free. If we continue in what God has already given us, we will be blessed, fulfilled, and safe!

◆ Chapter Two

JESUS CAME IN THE FLESH

"Beloved, do not believe every spirit, but test the spirits, whether they are of God; because many false prophets have gone out into the world. By this you know the Spirit of God: Every spirit that confesses that Jesus Christ has come in the flesh is of God, and every spirit that does not confess that Jesus Christ has come in the flesh is not of God. And this is the spirit of the Antichrist, which you have heard was coming, and is now already in the world" (1 John 4:1-3).

The Spirit of God has come to confess "Jesus came in the Flesh." Confess means to "agree with" or "say the same thing as." This means that everything the Spirit of God says and does, will always agree with *everything* Jesus said and did in the flesh!

"And the Word became flesh and dwelt among us, and we beheld His glory, the glory as of the only begotten of the Father, full of grace and truth" (John 1:14).

When Jesus came in the flesh, He brought the Word alive to us. Because of what He came to do, we can now look at His life and words, and begin to understand the whole Bible. Without the Word being made vivid and alive through Him, we cannot hope to properly grasp or understand the will of God.

In some churches, the revelation of Jesus Christ isn't taught or understood; therefore, the Word of God and will of God is still a mystery to them. They confess, "the will of God is mysterious. God works in mysterious ways and we will never know why. Man was never meant to know the entire will of God. It's beyond our comprehension."

This disagrees with the whole purpose of Jesus coming in the flesh. This reveals to me that some of us have trouble seeing the true revelation of Jesus Christ. This is a common problem in the Church. There is a simple answer when God doesn't seem to make sense: "LOOK AT JESUS."

God is no longer hidden if we look at Jesus. It is now possible for us to see the true character of God revealed in its entirety if we would only look at His Son. Once we see that the purpose and plan of God is completely made known through the life and words of Jesus in the flesh, then our discernment will be able to test many false spiritual manifestations.

JESUS DECLARED GOD'S TRUE CHARACTER

"No one has seen God at any time. The only begotten Son, who is in the bosom of the Father, He has declared Him" (John 1:18).

The Son has *declared* the Father's true character. "Declared" means that God was "manifested" to us through Jesus. In fact, this is the reason why one of the names given to Jesus was "Immanuel," which means, "God with us." God is no longer hidden from our understanding. His character and His Word have been made flesh and we can now open our Bibles and see Him in living color.

"And we know that the Son of God has come and has given

us an understanding, that we may know Him who is true; and we are in Him who is true, in His Son Jesus Christ. This is the true God and eternal life" (1 John 5:20).

We will continue to live in confusion until we realize that God is no longer invisible. He can now be seen through Jesus Christ!

"He (Jesus) is the image of the invisible God..." (Colossians 1:15).

The word image means "likeness;" therefore, we can see God's true likeness and image in Jesus.

"Who being the brightness of His glory and the express image of His person..." (Hebrews 1:3).

Jesus is the exact expression of God's character. Jesus came to reveal – not just a portion of God's character – but the entire revelation of His Father. He came in the flesh to reveal the fullness of God. People may ask, "But how can God, who is eternal, reveal Himself in flesh?" This was the mystery that Paul understood.

"...God was manifested in the flesh... Believed on in the world, Received up in glory" (1 Timothy 3:16).

"How that by revelation He made known to me the mystery (as I have briefly written already, by which, when you read, you may understand my knowledge in the mystery of Christ), which in other ages was not made known to the sons of men, as it has now been revealed by the Spirit to His holy apostles and prophets" (Ephesians 3:3-5).

IT IS NO LONGER A SECRET

God is no longer a mystery! His character is no longer hidden! His will is no longer shrouded in secrecy! Jesus has come in the flesh and we have beheld His full glory!

"For in Him dwells all the fullness of the Godhead bodily" (Colossians 2:9).

"For it pleased the Father that in Him all the fullness should dwell" (Colossians 1:19).

I once asked a fellow minister during a heated discussion, "Did God reveal Himself *totally* through Christ or did He reveal only a *portion* of His glory?" He couldn't answer me. Since then, I have realized that many of us cannot answer that question with a definite unwavering answer because we do not understand the revelation of Christ.

The Fullness of God Revealed

If we don't realize that the fullness of the Godhead was revealed in the earthly body of Christ, then we will not understand the true character of God and His Spirit. And if we don't understand the true character of God, then we will be easily misled by spiritual manifestations which do not agree with His character. In order to discern, we must understand, the revelation of God in Christ was complete!

"And the Word became flesh and dwelt among us, and we beheld His glory, the glory as of the only begotten of the Father, full of grace and truth" (John 1:14).

"No one has seen God at any time. The only begotten Son, who is in the bosom of the Father, He has declared Him" (John 1:18).

The word "glory" means to reveal the true opinion of someone. Jesus came to destroy all misconceptions falsely attached to His heavenly Father. If we have any wrong opinions about God, they will always be challenged when we take a good look at Jesus. He accurately showed us the true view of God's character!

Jesus also manifested and glorified the *name* of His Father. The Bible's use of names represented more than just titles. Names represented the entire character and every true attribute seen in Bible individuals. It represented everything which was associated with their name.

The name "Jesus" isn't just a title. It means "Jehovah saves" or "Jehovah is salvation." To understand His name, means to understand His character. But there is more to this. Jesus did not come to represent Himself. He came to represent His Father. Jesus revealed everything associated with his Father's name. He showed us, through His earthly ministry, the full meaning of His name – *Jesus – Jehovah is our salvation.*

"I have manifested Your name..." (John 17:6).

"The works that I do in My Father's name..." (John 10:25).

THE EXPRESS IMAGE OF GOD

Hebrews chapter one shows Jesus as the one true expression of God.

"He is the reflection of God's glory and the exact imprint of God's very being..." (Hebrews 1:3, NRSV).

"Who being the shining splendor of His glory, and the express image of His essence..." (Hebrews 1:3, Green's Literal Translation).

The word "essence" is a good word because Jesus truly was the "concentrate" of God's character. There is nothing more exact in all the world. He was the very essence of God!

Now, I have said all that to say this: In order to compare spiritual manifestations with truth, we have to realize that *truth is a person!*

THE RIGHT FOUNDATION

One minister from a neighboring town took me for coffee to discuss some of these issues. He was trying to convince me that God did things that are not found in the Bible. Instead of turning to the revelation of Jesus as the standard for truth, he turned to circumstances, traditions, and experiences to convince me that God does things that are mysterious and beyond our understanding.

I reminded him, "Jesus Christ is the exact expression of the will and image of God." I thought the minister might see that Jesus was the ultimate basis for truth.

All Christians should be able to reason that the truth was found in Jesus and therefore conclude that God has revealed Himself fully through His Son.

JOHN 21:25 MISUNDERSTANDING

But what really surprised me was his response to the testimony of Jesus. He said, "not everything Jesus did was recorded in the Bible." He explained, "I base this on John 21:25 which says, 'And there are also many other things which Jesus did, the which, if they should be written every one, I suppose that even the world itself could not contain the books that should be written.'"

There wasn't anything else I could say. If we couldn't build from the same foundation, then we could not dialogue any further.

I have had several discussions with my Pentecostal and Charismatic peers over these concepts. The same logic is used to defend extra-biblical signs and wonders. In defense of their views, several of my friends have misquoted this Scripture to me.

"And there are also many other things that Jesus did, which if they were written one by one, I suppose that even the world itself could not contain the books that would be written. Amen" (John 21:25).

They have used this Scripture to suggest that the character

of God was not totally revealed and cannot be limited to the written Word or the revelation of Christ.

It's Like a "DOS" Gateway

If you have ever used a computer, you know that as long as you stay within a written program, you are safe. When you make a mistake, the program tells you what you did wrong and offers you suggestions of how to return safely to your work. But within just about every computer program is a DOS gateway. Once you enter that gateway, you're no longer within a pre-written program. In DOS, mistakes can be very costly. This is the domain for those who wish to write their own programs.

The misuse of John 21:25 is like a DOS gateway. Whoever thinks he can go beyond the written Word to defend his own doctrines is in grave danger. By misusing this Scripture, he begins writing his own program. He raises his own standard. (Besides, the statement found in John 21:25 applies in particular to the book of John, not to the entire Bible.)

We need to stand on solid ground. Jesus is the entire character of the Almighty God focused and concentrated into one person. This is our firm foundation. Everything else is sand.

Two Ditches

As I am exposing some of my own pseudo-Christ Charismatic training, I also want you to know that the revelation of Jesus Christ challenges some of our more traditional evangelical beliefs as well.

Across the whole spectrum of the Church we can find doctrines which go beyond Scripture. Some of our more popular denominations are just as vulnerable as their Charismatic counterparts for not using the doctrine of Christ as the foundation for what they believe. Perhaps they do it because they highly regard their founding fathers and would not question them; or perhaps, like the Charismatics, they have not been presented with the true revelation of Christ. Nevertheless, there remains denominational strongholds that have to be broken through. If ministers returned to the pursuit of truth, at the expense of some of their man-made traditions, they would inevitably face resistance.

They may not realize it, but sometimes denominational standards are sprinkled with as much influence from the spirit of Antichrist as the "flakiness" of the Charismatics. Keep in mind though, the spirit of Antichrist is not opposed to religion or denominations. Antichrist influence is simply opposed to the *full revelation of God through Christ in the flesh* – that's all.

There is nothing more fundamental or foundational in all of Christianity than the revelation of Christ!

The Other Ditch

Full Gospel or Charismatic leaders have to venture beyond the doctrine of Christ in order to defend their man-made doctrines. They become very good at mishandling and misquoting Bible verses.

On the false premise of John 21:25 and other connected teachings, I have witnessed preachers declare and believe whole-heartedly that they can do more things than Jesus did and do them better. This becomes very evident when the spiritual manifestations, which they promote in their ministries, are different than the manifestations found in Jesus' ministry. This is founded on the assumption that Jesus opened up the opportunity to do what He couldn't do. This too reveals the influence of carnal, anti-Christ thought.

"For many deceivers have gone out into the world who do not confess (agree with) Jesus Christ as coming in the flesh. This

Chapter Two

is a deceiver and an antichrist" (2 John 1:7).

"Whoever transgresses and does not abide in the doctrine of Christ does not have God. He who abides in the doctrine of Christ has both the Father and the Son" (2 John 1:9).

John's use of the word "transgress" is a little different in this setting because we usually use the word "sin" in its place. "Transgress" fits into this context because it actually means "to go beyond or step aside." John's warning must be understood. He is teaching this in order to keep us from going beyond the doctrine of Christ. Everything Jesus said and did in His body is the ultimate standard for truth!

Leaders and Christians under the influence of the spirit of Antichrist will not openly confess or admit that the complete revelation of the Word of God was revealed through the life of Jesus Christ. If ministers made a stand for truth, they might not be accepted within their own traditional denominations. They would progress into scriptural knowledge which might jeopardize their licenses and their memberships. But that is the risk they may have to take in order to become true leaders in the Body of Christ. Every believer is entitled to the reward of the ever-increasing knowledge of the revelation of Christ!

It is like entering the strait gate. It seems so small at first. It seems to limit us. But on the other side is the vast knowledge of God and His Word. There is an abundance of understanding set aside for us *within* the simple but powerful revelation of Christ.

◆ Chapter Three

TEST THE SPIRITS

The message is very simple, "We are not supposed to believe everything we see and hear simply because it sounds spiritual or because it's in the Church." We are counseled to use discernment.

And based on 1 John 4:1-3, we are to understand that every spirit which confesses that Jesus Christ came in the flesh is of God and every spirit which does not is the spirit of Antichrist.

"Beloved, do not believe every spirit, but test the spirits, whether they are of God; because many false prophets have gone out into the world. By this you know the Spirit of God: Every spirit that confesses that Jesus Christ has come in the flesh is of God, and every spirit that does not confess that Jesus Christ has come in the flesh is not of God. And this is the *spirit of the Antichrist*, which you have heard was coming, and is now already in the world" (1 John 4:1-3).

The Church isn't discerning the spirits of Antichrist like it should because we have misunderstood the meaning of this Scripture. Christians have assumed that it would be easy to discern spirits, but without understanding the true meaning of these verses, the difference between the Spirit of God and the spirit of the Antichrist will not be properly discerned. What we should be judging is not the obvious, blatant, black lies around us but simply a subtle lack of truth. And yet, how can we expose a subtle lie if we don't know the truth ourselves?

There is something very important we must see in this phrase, "every spirit that *does not* confess... is the spirit of Antichrist." What the spirit of Antichrist openly confesses is not as dangerous or hard to discern as what *they don't say*. This is why discerning the spirit of Antichrist is not as obvious as we've assumed.

"Every spirit that confesses that Jesus Christ has come in the flesh is of God, and every spirit that does not confess that Jesus Christ has come in the flesh is not of God" (1 John 4:2-3).

The word "confess" carries with it the meaning of agreement. What the Holy Spirit says and does will always "agree" with everything Jesus said and did in the flesh.

We must be careful. The spirit of Antichrist won't always openly *disagree* with what Jesus did in the flesh, but may, more likely, subtly *neglect* to agree with Him. It is not the obvious words of disagreement that signal to us the presence of false doctrine.

No Discernment Needed For the Obvious

In fact, it doesn't take much discernment at all to see the blatantly obvious. It is not hard to discern those who openly and outwardly deny that Jesus came in the flesh. Cults and religions which openly deny that Jesus was the Son of God or those who openly deny He was in fact God with us, are of little threat to the Church.

It is the subtle soft words of emptiness *within* the Church which need to be exposed first. Those which do not openly testify of Jesus' true character. Actually, the *lack* of words of agreement are the most dangerous and the most deceptive.

Just because words spoken by Christian leaders sound spiritual doesn't mean they should be heeded. The spirits of Antichrist within the Church will confess many spiritual things. They will even quote much of the Bible. They will perform signs and wonders which fascinate the soul. They will appear as apostles, prophets, and pastors, but they will avoid pointing us to the fact that Jesus Christ was the complete revelation of God's will and character in the flesh.

The words and miracles of the Holy Spirit will always agree with the concepts Jesus revealed in the flesh. Ministers under the influence of the spirit of Antichrist will not openly confess this. They will usually confess many spiritual sounding words and do many awesome looking things within the Church. However, these messages and manifestations will clash with the revelation of Christ because they are empty of the Living Word and the Gospel of Christ.

TEST THE SPIRITS WITHIN THE CHURCH

"Test the spirits, whether they are of God..." (1 John 4:1).

John the Apostle is writing this letter to Christians. He is not talking about testing or looking outside the boundaries of the Church. We need to take his advice and test the spirits *within* the Church. Some will call our obedient testing, "unbelief." Some will call us "miracle haters." But don't be discouraged. Go ahead and test!

A true prophet (leader) won't be shaken when tested according to the Word, but a false prophet will get very defensive and nervous.

Don't be afraid to examine miracles either. A true miracle of God won't fall apart simply because we examine it – but a lying wonder sure will.

Chapter Three

In these last days, Christians need to walk in sharper perception than ever before.

"For false christs and false prophets will rise and show great signs and wonders to deceive, if possible, even the elect" (Matthew 24:24).

We are dealing with something more subtle and devious than we first thought. There is a need to scripturally expose antichrist doctrines because they are well hidden within our Christian traditions. How many of us would easily admit that it's possible for us to be deceived? We usually consider this possibility to be very remote.

The Bible clearly teaches us that the last days are going to be a time of great deception, a great falling away, and a heaping up of teachers that tickle the ears. So why do we go on as if these Scriptures don't apply to us?

As Evangelical Christians, we are quick to point to the defective judgment of the Charismatics; but we are slow to challenge our own man-made beliefs. Conversely, the Word of Faith leaders willingly preach about the unbelief of the Fundamentalists, but fail to evaluate their own extremes. So why do we assume that antichrist teachings and attitudes are only going to deceive those who are outside our church group? We justify our beliefs by comparing our doctrines with those of our own camp. We have failed to compare ourselves to the doctrine of Christ.

If deception was so easy to detect, then why would the Bible include so much information about it? Why would Jesus warn us about the deception in the last days by saying, "take heed, watch out, and beware?" Wouldn't we be better off if we listened to Him?

I Was Blind

There was a time when I was blind: I couldn't see what I was doing wrong. A person who is deceived is blinded by ignorance.

That is why lack of knowledge is the same as darkness and deception. The lack of the light and the absence of truth equate spiritual blindness.

But Now I See

The true revelation of Christ was the light and knowledge that set me free. In fact, the kind of knowledge that the Devil is most afraid of is the revelation of Jesus Christ. Jesus as "light" not only reveals truth, but also exposes every hidden, ungodly lie. As long as Christians are steadily increasing in the knowledge of Christ, they will grow in righteous judgment, gain sharp discernment, and successfully expose the spirit of Antichrist.

Empty, Empty, Empty

Throughout the Bible, there are prophetic clues which identify false prophets, false teachers, false signs, lying wonders, and everything connected with deception. One of them is the concept; "empty." When I studied false prophets, I repeatedly found that emptiness was connected with false prophecies and false teachings. Therefore, emptiness is one of the biggest enemies of God's people. In the last days, Christians will need to be filled with the Living Word of God in order to discern the empty. Empty Christians will not be able to discern empty doctrine. Christians will successfully discern the counterfeit only when they are filled with the genuine.

The Holy Spirit has come to glorify Jesus Christ and teach us truth. But the unholy spirit of Antichrist has come to magnify himself and beguile us with emptiness and vain imaginations. The goal of the Devil is to replace and substitute the truth of the Gospel with empty spiritual experiences and divination. He won't be able to do it as long as we are established in the knowledge of the Word – especially the Word made alive through the revelation of Christ!

HEALING – FOR OR AGAINST

One of the most sensitive areas of doctrine in the Church is the subject of healing. The spirit of Antichrist doesn't readily confess or agree that Jesus revealed the perfect will of God concerning healing; but, nevertheless, Jesus, through His life and words in the flesh, revealed everything God wanted us to know about healing.

As He walked the earth, He healed every sick person who came to Him by faith. He then commanded His disciples to go and do the same.

A preacher who is under the influence of a spirit of Antichrist won't openly refute or publicly agree with scriptural healing. But he may prefer to bypass it, not talk about it, or try to surpass it. He may choose to talk about something else, especially if it sounds spiritual. If put under pressure about the subject, he may quote as many out-of-context Bible examples as he can find.

On the extra-biblical side of the scale, he may use examples based on stories from people's experiences. On the more traditional side, he may use his own interpretations of Job's captivity or Paul's thorn. The point I want you to see in all of this is that people under the influence of wrong doctrines will avoid the life of Jesus Christ. Only Jesus can challenge *all* of our false ideas about how God works.

I don't think the book of Job or the subject of Paul's thorn will ever make sense to a Christian until they understand that Jesus Christ is the solid foundation for everything the Bible says. Without the proper foundation, the book of Job will not come alive. Without accurate revelation based on Jesus' life, the subject of Paul's thorn will seem to disagree with other parts of the Bible or give us the idea that God is an inconsistent dictator.

We will never understand the book of Job as a book of deliverance until we realize Jesus Christ is the book of Job made alive. Jesus is the Word of God made flesh. He is the whole Bible made reality! He's the most accurate interpretation of it all. He is the key that unlocks all of its hidden treasures. The will of God has been revealed in its entirety through the life of Jesus! It is a complete revelation. There is nothing missing.

Preachers who are holding to a doctrine which is influenced by the spirit of Antichrist may not openly refute these concepts and facts, but the truth may be mysteriously absent from their doctrine.

If the Devil can't keep a preacher captive or contained by the traditions of men through unbelief, then he will try to lead him beyond the doctrine of Christ. The Devil is kept busy either trying to hold us back or push us beyond the revelation of Christ.

Holding Back or Being Pushy

If the Devil discovers that the truth about healing is being realized in a believer and he can't steal it from him, then the next tactic is to try to lead him *beyond* proper teaching, into variations of healing. Inner healing of the past, falling on the floor, healing through music, and deliverance through strange experiences are good examples of this in the Church today.

False teachers, who go beyond proper doctrine, portray God as one who has unlimited ways to heal or deliver His people. That's how we get away with so many strange methods of ministry. It is as if Jesus never came and established the standard of how God works.

We go beyond the standard of Jesus' life to say that God heals using strange methods. "The stranger the manifestation,"

Chapter Three

we reason, "the more probable that it's God." "After all," we surmise, "Jesus put mud on the blind man's eyes and spit on the tongue of the man who was dumb." We have made a new doctrine, "The never-been-done-before is the sign of a true miracle of God." We don't understand why Jesus used the mud and what parable language was behind it or why He healed the way He did. We carnally think, "Jesus did it to be different."

What we should realize is miracles which have never been done before could easily be classified as antichrist manifestations, because they do not agree with the miracles Jesus performed while in the flesh. The kind of miracles which do not confess that Jesus came and performed the whole and perfect will of God in the flesh need to be exposed (1 John 4:1-3).

NEW MIRACLES

New signs and wonders confess that Jesus *didn't* do *all* the works of God while He was on the earth. They don't realize that those who confess, "God is doing a new thing," are really saying, "God didn't reveal everything He wanted to show us through His Son." Preachers who defend strange new manifestations will even quote Isaiah 43:19; "Behold, I will do a new thing, Now it shall spring forth; Shall you not know it?" What they fail to realize is Jesus is the fulfillment of that "new thing." He is the source and fulfillment of every prophetic promise. Something else they don't realize is, even though Jesus was the manifestation of that new thing, He Himself still had to agree with the established, written will of God.

Jesus was the written Word made flesh. This means He and His Father did not invent new miracles as He ministered to people. He only performed miracles which agreed with the written Word. In fact, all the miracles Jesus performed in His earthy ministry were already established in the Word. They may seem hidden in the Old Testament, because of our lack of understanding. But He revealed them. He did *not* do His own thing.

"For I have come down from heaven, not to do My own will, but the will of Him who sent Me" (John 6:38).

Jesus did not come in His own name. He came in the name of His Father. He didn't do new miracles. He did the miracles which were already recorded in God's Word.

New Erroneous Concepts

In the Gospels, some people who claimed to love God, were not receiving Jesus; therefore, He exposed their rejection of Him as a clear rejection of God. He was saying, "If I had done new miracles or brought them a new concept of God, then they would have had every right to reject Me."

The Word of God was His standard! He only performed miracles found in the Word of God!

Some would speculate that Jesus was so led by the Spirit that God continually sent Jesus special instructions commanding Him to perform new miracles using never-been-done-before styles and methods. But that is not the case.

If we understand that Jesus was the Word made flesh, then we will understand that He also willingly limited His ministry to the standards of the Word.

God the Father voluntarily limited Himself in the same way in the Old Testament. Although God was all-powerful and all-knowing, He limited Himself to His own Covenant and His Word. He was known as the covenant-keeping God. Everything that happened in the Old Testament was established by covenants between God and man. There were no loose threads – no hidden agendas. God had given man His Word in order to become accessible and predictable. He willingly bound Himself to His promises. Therefore, if we realize that God's Word is eternal; we will see that God will never do anything or be anything beyond the Word He has already given to man.

HE PERFORMED THE WORD

Jesus operated His earthly ministry the same way. He willingly performed and submitted Himself to the Word. He was the entire will of God put into a living body so that we could clearly see it. There was nothing that Jesus did or taught that was entirely new. He simply made the existing Word easier to understand as He fulfilled it.

Here is one example: The feeding of the thousands with the fishes and the loaves was simply the same manifestation as other miracles of multiplied food found in the Old Testament.

"Then a man came from Baal Shalisha, and brought the man of God bread of the firstfruits, twenty loaves of barley bread, and newly ripened grain in his knapsack. And he said, "Give it to the people, that they may eat. But his servant said, "What? Shall I set this before one hundred men?" He said again, "Give it to the people, that they may eat; for thus says the Lord: 'They shall eat and have some left over.' So he set it before them; and they ate and had some left over, according to the word of the Lord" (2 Kings 4:42-44).

This concept rings true throughout Jesus' ministry. Jesus didn't do anything beyond the written will of God. He didn't invent miracles on His own. He simply revealed what was already established by God. He made the Word live. He was the perfect expression of God's character.

Now it's our turn. We are called to glorify and reveal Jesus. We too are limited to perform only the known will of God. We are to be like Christ in everything we say and do. If we are unlike Him in any way, especially in spiritual manifestations, and are not corrected, we will become anti-Christ.

It's very simple: God is exactly like His Word, Jesus was exactly like His Father, and we are to be exactly like Jesus. Our ultimate goal is to know Him intimately and to be willingly changed into His image.

Romans 8:29 "For whom He foreknew, He also predestined to be conformed to the image of His Son, that He might be the firstborn among many brethren"

Some find this too limiting for them. But consider the fact that we have not yet manifested all the miracles that Jesus did. For many of us, we have yet to raise the dead, heal the sick, or even rebuke the Pharisees. Is there a shortage of miracles, signs and wonders to perform, even if we limit ourselves to those performed by Jesus?

We as believers, have become naive. We are either open to strange new miracles and manifestations or we are in the other ditch, totally opposed to signs and wonders. Both of these stances are common because we haven't patterned ourselves after Jesus.

ROCK OF SAFETY

Jesus is the Rock of our salvation. The word "rock" can also be translated "fortress of security, refuge, or safe stronghold." The revelation of Jesus is the fortress of our salvation. The more we know about Him, the safer we will be. Remaining in the doctrine of Christ means safety. Going beyond the "Rock" is risky. We become vulnerable only when we leave the fortress. When outside the stronghold of safety, we become easy prey for the enemy. (For more on this concept, read *Jesus Christ – Solid Rock*, by Ted Brooks. See Resources at the back of this book.)

"Whoever transgresses (goes beyond) and does not abide in the doctrine of Christ does not have God. He who abides in the doctrine of Christ has both the Father and the Son" (2 John 1:9).

Chapter Three

If we go beyond the doctrine of Christ, how can we say that God is with us? The doctrine of Christ isn't just what He taught. It includes everything He did and everything He represented in the flesh. He said, "eat my flesh." This means to take in His doctrine (which includes His life and ministry) and to devour His Word.

Jesus is the truth about God made alive in the flesh. He is the foundation for all truth upon which we are to be established. If we go beyond revealed truth, we will no longer be safe. Jesus is our firm foundation – all other ground is sinking sand.

COMMON ERRORS

There are many things that the Church believes and practices which are beyond the doctrine of Christ. We are always quick to attack the Charismatic arm of the Church in this regard, but the Fundamental arm is just as vulnerable.

Some Fundamentalists are hasty to label Charismatics as "mystic," but fail to see their own mistakes. They are quick to expose Charismatic mysticism. I have read many anti-charismatic authors who say things like, "They twist the Bible to fit their theology and their experiences. And sometimes, they ignore the Bible altogether. Their brand of Christianity is a mixture of mysticism and pragmatism. They exalt their feelings above traditional Christian thought. Their feelings have become more important to them than objective facts."

I agree with this definition, but authors like this fail to apply the same thinking to their own mysticism. For in dealing with some of these issues, they too exalt their experiences to justify their beliefs. For instance, when dealing with the subject of healing, they ask, "Does God still heal?" And then they will base their theology on a statement like, "I prayed for sick and nothing happened, therefore, I know healing is passed away."

If we think God is saying "no" simply because the circumstances look impossible, aren't we being just as mystic as someone who bases their beliefs on a silly vision? To form a doctrine about God's character, based on an empty experience, is just as anti-christ as any other doctrine which doesn't agree with what Jesus did in the flesh.

Let's be fair. All experiences are subject to discernment. If Fundamentalists are going to expose mysticism, why don't they expose their own first and leave the Charismatic arm of the Church to do it's own cleansing? We have all fallen short of the stature and standard of Christ – Charismatics, and Fundamentalists alike.

Why is it so important that we deal with the ultra-sovereignty doctrine in a discernment book which has been written to expose Charismatic doctrines? It is simply because the Charismatics have borrowed this doctrine and have used it for advancements into new doctrines. The Charismatics have skillfully used the doctrine of the ultra-sovereign God to promote the Autonomous God of their revivals. "God can do anything He wants," is the byword for today's bogus revival meetings.

If God wants to heal a woman's neck by shaking her head back and forth for several hours during a revival service, then who are we to question it?

Most Christian dare not doubt a strange manifestation for fear of speaking out against God. Why? We respect the doctrine of the ultra-sovereign God. We believe His divine will cannot be questioned. Or it is often said that we are finite people questioning the actions of an infinite God. "After all," we've been told, "We can't put God in a box."

We fail to realize that God Himself is not greater than His own promises nor does He have the kind of character that would try to venture beyond His own Word.

Chapter Three

He will not do foolish things nor make us look foolish because that is not part of His nature. "But," someone might say, "God uses the foolish things of this world." How true this would be, if they were describing the attitude of the world toward the cross of Jesus Christ. But by foolishness, they are hinting that the silly gestures, the animal antics, and the crazy body charades, which are manifesting at various revival meetings around the country, are from God. "Because," we reason, "God uses the foolish things to confound the wise."

Why do we accept animal gestures as prophetic manifestations in revival meetings today? We seem to think that these antics are parabolic in nature.

We fail to understand God's parable language. Therefore, we invent our own parables and think it is on the same level as God's divine lessons. We manufacture our own manifestations and say; "God is speaking to us." When a man gets down on the floor on his hands and knees and roars like a lion, we think it is scriptural because the Bible mentions something somewhere about a lion. We are truly making a leap. And because we don't understand God's parable language, we don't suspect that our actions are foreign to biblical thought. In actuality, we aren't even close.

We are being beguiled into accepting spiritual foolishness because we forget that the prophets were sent to remind the Children of Israel to return to the Word of God. None of the parabolic gestures that the prophets had to perform were new to those who knew the Word. All of their actions and words were prophetic because they were once again speaking and declaring God's Word. Nothing they had to say was new or mysterious.

Today's revival manifestations are not reminding us to return to God's Word. In fact, I would venture to say, I have heard more sermons that belittle those who hold onto the Word, than at any other time in my life. And revival preachers love to emphasize these kind of messages. Return to the Word? On the contrary, many revival leaders can be heard saying, "Put your Bibles away, put your theology aside, and don't question what God is doing."

BALAAM'S DONKEY

These so-called prophetic manifestations are usually defended as biblical in some way. For instance, some people who are confronted with how silly they look as they roar like a lion or bay like a donkey, provide us with a common response: "Well, if God can speak through Balaam's donkey, He can speak through me."

This brings up an interesting point because God did not speak through Balaam's donkey. God opened the donkey's mouth and she spoke for herself (Numbers 22).

This may be closer to the truth when dealing with these foolish antics which are done in the name of the Spirit. These folks, who think that God is speaking through them by crowing like a rooster at the front of the Church, are simply opening their mouths and speaking for themselves. The silly antics alone are the telltale fruit of false seeds planted in the hearts of carnal Christians. The fruit of foolish doctrine is finally coming into full bloom.

THE GOD OF REVIVAL

While both Fundamentalist and Charismatic camps fight with each other, they fail to see that their views of God are very similar. For both portray God as completely in control of everything which happens in their lives. We've been told with hypnotic repetition by both camps, "God works in mysterious ways."

God is not mysterious. He is not inventing new miracles and manifestations each new day of every new revival. God is not portrayed like that in the Bible. He is exactly like His Son. There is nothing about Him which is hidden, because Jesus completely revealed His Father to us.

"For in Him dwells all the fullness of the Godhead bodily..." (Colossians 2:9).

LET'S BE FAIR

If we are going to challenge Charismatic doctrine, let us be fair. There are some standard, traditional beliefs within the Church, which should also be questioned. Once again, the revelation of Christ must have the preeminence – not our denominational standards.

By looking at Jesus we can truly see and understand God's true character. "And we know that the Son of God has come and has given us an understanding, that we may know Him who is true; and we are in Him who is true, in His Son Jesus Christ. This is the true God and eternal life" (1 John 5:20).

FAITH IS KNOWING GOD

True faith is knowing God through His Son. In fact, faith is knowing the true will and character of God as perfectly revealed through the knowledge of Christ. We'll trust Him when we know Him. The more we know Him, the more we'll trust Him.

WAS JESUS' MINISTRY INCOMPLETE?

If God is doing new things today, that were never seen in Jesus' ministry, then the revelation of Jesus was incomplete. This is exactly what the Devil wants us to think. If he can deceive us into thinking that God is doing things today which were never seen in Jesus' ministry, then the Devil will successfully exalt himself in the Church through false signs and wonders.

"Let no one deceive you by any means; for that Day will not come unless the falling away comes first, and the man of sin is revealed, the son of perdition, who opposes and exalts himself above all that is called God or that is worshiped, so that he sits as God in the temple of God, showing himself that he is God" (2 Thessalonians 2:3-4).

Satan can only have his way if he can remove or replace Jesus as the only true image of God. That is why he is called "Antichrist."

He is trying to bring false concepts of God into the Church through signs, wonders and false doctrines via leaders and teachers in the Church. If we don't test these manifestations and doctrines, they will lead us astray.

"For false christs and false prophets will rise and show great signs and wonders to deceive, if possible, even the elect" (Matthew 24:24).

This is why every spirit, every message, every miracle, and every manifestation must be tested. Do the concepts of God expressed through today's miracles agree with the concepts of God revealed in Jesus? If they don't, we have every right to cast them down as vain imaginations.

"Casting down arguments and every high thing that exalts itself against the knowledge of God, bringing every thought into captivity to the obedience of Christ..." (2 Corinthians 10:5).

Jesus is the revealed knowledge of God. Every thought about God – who He is and what He's doing in the Church – must be subjected to examination in that light. We can bring every one of those thoughts into the obedience of Christ.

◆ Chapter Four

SIGNS AND WONDERS

"And the devil said to Him, "If You are the Son of God, command this stone to become bread" (Luke 4:3).

There it is – *"If"* – the biggest word in the Devil's vocabulary.

The Devil is still saying the same thing to all of God's sons and daughters. "If you are a son or daughter of God, prove it. Lets see some signs and wonders. If you truly are a minister of the Gospel, let's see something supernatural."

The Church has fallen for this one. We have believed that Jesus came to prove His "deity" through powerful works. We've been convinced that Jesus performed signs and wonders in order to prove to people that He was the Son of God. This is where we have plunged into error.

Jesus didn't come to promote Himself. He came to exalt and reveal His Father's true character.

No, Jesus didn't have to prove anything, because faith is not based on what you see. Faith is based on the reality of God and His Living Word! Since Jesus was the Living Word, He was seeking out those who had faith in Him or those who would hear and obey His words. He was not using signs and wonders to promote Himself. He was exalting God. Signs and wonders occurred in the New Testament as people believed in Jesus as the Living Word.

If faith was based on signs and wonders, then Jesus shouldn't have walked away from Nazareth because of their unbelief. He should have wowed them with more signs and wonders, proving to them that He was the Messiah. He shouldn't have wept over Jerusalem because they wouldn't believe.

If the purpose of signs and wonders was to make them believe He should have marched right down there and showed them more miracles. Jesus shouldn't have let people walk away in their unbelief.

"Paul Shouldn't Have Walked Away"

If the goal was to convince people to believe by using miracles, then Paul shouldn't have walked away from unbelieving towns and synagogues. He should have persevered against the resistance and confirmed what he was preaching with signs and wonders.

No, the faith in the good news had to come first. It always has and it always will.

When the Devil tempted Jesus to turn stones into bread, Jesus answered him, saying, "It is written, That man shall not live by bread alone, but by every word of God" (Luke 4:4).

We should answer the Devil the same way Jesus did. "I am not going to live on outward signs and wonders. I'm going to live by the Living Word of God."

The Holy Spirit was sent to confirm the Word of God in those who believed in the Gospel, the power of His Word. He was not sent to dwell in us to put on a big show to prove to unbelieving people that we have the power of God.

"And these signs will follow those who believe: In My name

Chapter Four

they will cast out demons; they will speak with new tongues; they will take up serpents; and if they drink anything deadly, it will by no means hurt them; they will lay hands on the sick, and they will recover" (Mark 16:17-18).

The Holy Spirit confirms the Word we preach only when people believe. Signs and wonders are not for the purpose of making people believe or proving God is real. This is where the Devil has been able to get the Church off course.

It seems the goal has become to get people healed, delivered or at least feeling better with whatever method is popular at the time. We appear to have little or no regard for the kind of method we use, even if it does bypass faith in Jesus.

SEEKING SENSATIONS

The Devil doesn't care if you feel a sensation of healing or not. He doesn't care if you end up feeling better. All he cares about is bypassing Jesus! If he can get people to bypass Jesus on their way to comfort or relief, he will do so. And after that, he will continue to keep them captive through soulish experiences. If he can convince Christians to seek these sensations, then the Devil will find it easier to replace God and exalt his own image in the Church.

We must remember that the Devil is not only anti-Jesus, but he is also pseudo-Jesus. This means he replaces Jesus whenever he can – usually by misleading people through false deeds done in Jesus' name. In fact, the Devil is very interested in appearing benevolent, kind, and generous. Satan wants to use the name of Jesus as a covering to manifest his own brand of miracles. This shouldn't shock us. Many false things are done in the Church under the covering of the name of Jesus.

"Many will say to Me in that day, 'Lord, Lord, have we not prophesied in Your name, cast out demons in Your name, and done many wonders in Your name?" (Matthew 7:22).

Jesus warned us about being signs-and-wonders-conscious.

"For false christs and false prophets will rise and show great signs and wonders to deceive, if possible, even the elect" (Matthew 24:24).

The false prophet will have difficulty in deceiving Christians who are honestly seeking truth. But he will find it easier to deceive those who are carnally seeking experiences, signs, and wonders.

The carnal Christian won't believe unless he sees with his physical eyes. That is why he is so easily deceived by what he sees.

The carnal Christian believes and follows signs and wonders, even if they are demonic, because he won't read his Bible. On the other hand, the strong believer has faith because he sees the true character of God as he reads his Bible. True signs and wonders will only follow those who believe the Living Word.

True and False Prophets

"If there arises among you a prophet or a dreamer of dreams, and he gives you a sign or a wonder, and the sign or the wonder comes to pass, of which he spoke to you, saying, 'Let us go after other gods'—which you have not known—'and let us serve them,' you shall not listen to the words of that prophet or that dreamer of dreams..." (Deuteronomy 13:1-3).

Signs and wonders are not the only test of a true prophet. With a little Bible study, it becomes obvious that both true and false prophets produce signs and wonders.

If a prophet points you to Jesus Christ as the true image of God and causes you to repent from following false concepts, then that prophet is probably from God. But, if a prophet leads you to a different image of God other than the one revealed in

Jesus, then that prophet is probably influenced by anti-Christ doctrine.

Since most signs and wonders are attributed to the Holy Spirit, we must remember that the Holy Spirit has not come to do anything else but glorify Jesus Christ. The Holy Spirit has not come to bring attention to himself, nor has He come to the earth to establish His own ministry! He is here to help us glorify Jesus and lead us into truth!

False Anointing

If a preacher indicates to us that he carries a special anointing to set people free and if that anointing or spiritual experience, he is promoting appears to bypass faith in the name of the true Jesus, then we need to be on guard. Not because freedom is bad, but because the experience he is trying to sell is probably anti-Jesus.

We must remember, the Devil isn't anti-religion or anti-spiritual experience, he is anti-Jesus and hence his name is "ANTICHRIST."

Whenever he can help people feel a sensation of freedom in their soul and cause them to bypass true freedom in Christ, he will.

True Freedom Comes Via the Word

Good Bible teaching has taken a back seat to personal prophetic counseling because of our focus on feelings. Counseling satisfies the need for special attention – whereas teaching does not. Being a disciple in a group with the rest of the believers does not get individual attention so we have invented a new brand of counseling. However, this is not what Jesus meant when He taught us about making disciples. Today's concept of helping people feel better about themselves is not the true path to freedom.

"Then Jesus said to those Jews who believed Him, "If you abide in My word, you are My disciples indeed" (John 8:31).

We must understand – freedom isn't a feeling. Freedom comes with the knowledge of the truth!

"And you shall know the truth, and the truth shall make you free" (John 8:32).

If the Devil can cause us to bypass truth on our way to freedom, then he will continue to keep us in bondage.

In some people, it's almost as if the soulish sensation of freedom is their ultimate goal and it doesn't matter how they get it. The problem is when they bypass Jesus on their way to freedom, they lose the true healing and receive a counterfeit. Of course, this is all done in the name of the "anointing."

Our Own Version of Freedom

We as Charismatics repeatedly made this blunder. The freedom we pursued was linked more to how we felt after a service than to what we learned. Even if we learned something new, we rated its importance by how "moving" the subject was. More importantly was how entertaining the talented preacher was as he made his presentation. If the preacher presented vital truth to us in a monotone or boring manner, we would have missed it.

The anointing of God will never make a believer do or experience anything which isn't founded in the ministry of Jesus, because the Holy Spirit hasn't come to do His own thing.

This misunderstanding is founded upon a major misnomer in Charismatic circles. The Holy Spirit is promoted as an independent individual within the Godhead. This, of course, is partially true. But this teaching goes a little further and says that the Holy Spirit works independently and manifests miracles which were never seen in Jesus' ministry. Therefore they use the concept of the Holy Spirit as an independent member of the God-

Chapter Four

head to substantiate extra-biblical miracles and experiences. The Holy Spirit is promoted as active in His own unique ministry by manifesting new extra-biblical phenomena. This is not a true picture of the Spirit of God.

The Holy Spirit has come to help us understand and learn about the miracles that He helped Jesus do. What the Holy Spirit anointed Jesus to do, has to become the eternal standard for every single one of us. If we determine to make that revelation our never-changing-standard, then we will see through a lot of today's spiritual foolishness.

"How God anointed Jesus of Nazareth with the Holy Spirit and with power, who went about doing good and healing all who were oppressed by the devil, for God was with Him" (Acts 10:38).

The Holy Spirit has been sent to lead believers into truth. He will never bypass the truth He revealed in Christ.

"But when the Helper comes, whom I shall send to you from the Father, the Spirit of truth who proceeds from the Father, He will testify of Me" (John 15:26).

"However, when He, the Spirit of truth, has come, He will guide you into all truth; for He will not speak on His own authority, but whatever He hears He will speak; and He will tell you things to come. "He will glorify Me, for He will take of what is Mine and declare it to you" (John 16:13-14).

◆ Chapter Five

THE DEVIL WANTS ZION

"Stand against the wiles of the devil" (Ephesians 6:11). We will be better equipped to stand against the wiles of the Devil, if we come to a better understanding of the Devil's ultimate goals.

He was originally cast out of Heaven because he coveted God's throne. It seems he still hasn't learned his lesson. Many Christians tend to forget that Satan continues to seek the center of attention in the congregation of the Lord. He continues to be jealous of God and wants to be worshipped like Him.

He still wants to be God in the temple of God. He doesn't want to fight us to gain that position; in fact, he doesn't have to fight us. All he has to do is deceive us. He's not out to fight God either. He has already tried that and it didn't work. So, he would rather use trickery. His ultimate goal is not to appear as our enemy, but to take God's place.

Some people may wonder, "Why is the Devil trying to infiltrate the Church? Why doesn't he just settle for the false religions of the world? Why does he want to be worshipped by Christians? I thought we were his adversaries."

Chapter Five

The false religions of the world are not the Devil's ultimate quest. He wants the Church. He has always wanted the Church – right from the beginning! The Bible reveals some very interesting things about Lucifer and his quest.

"You (Lucifer) were the anointed cherub who covers; I established you; You were on the holy mountain of God; You walked back and forth in the midst of fiery stones" (Ezekiel 28:14).

The holy mountain of God is a picture of Zion and the Church. This is where God is worshipped. Lucifer was on the mountain with God until he desired God's throne. He was cast out of Heaven, but that did not deter him. He still thinks he can acquire God's place.

"How you are fallen from heaven, O Lucifer... For you have said in your heart: 'I will ascend into heaven, I will exalt my throne above the stars of God; I will also sit on the mount of the congregation On the farthest sides of the north; I will ascend above the heights of the clouds, I will be like the Most High'" (Isaiah 14:12-14).

He wants Zion, because it is the dwelling place of God both in Heaven and in the earth. This is why he brings deception into the Church. The Devil knows that he will be pushed aside as a small nuisance or a mere inconvenience when Christians worship the true image of God as revealed through Jesus Christ.

A False Concept of Christ

The only way that the Devil can infiltrate the Church is by presenting it a false concept of Christ. If he can succeed in placing a false image of God within the Church via false signs and wonders, then he will receive the worship of the congregation and assume God's place.

"(The Devil) who opposes and exalts himself above all that is called God or that is worshipped, so that he sits as God in the temple of God, showing himself that he is God" (2 Thessalonians 2:4).

The Devil wants to live in the dwelling place of God known as the Church because it is the only genuine place of worship. The cults cannot offer him this claim.

The Devil's temptation of Jesus revealed the Devil's true colors, "Therefore, if You will worship before me, all will be Yours." And Jesus answered and said to him, "Get behind Me, Satan! For it is written, 'You shall worship the Lord your God, and Him only you shall serve'" (Luke 4:7).

The Devil just can't seem to give up. The only way to stop him is to remain grounded in the revelation of Christ. The Devil cannot receive any worship from those who are committed to the Lord as their God nor from those who have made a commitment to honor Jesus Christ as their Messiah and King!

◆ Chapter Six

BEWARE THE FALSE PROPHET

"Beware of false prophets, who come to you in sheep's clothing, but inwardly they are ravenous wolves" (Matthew 7:15-20).

Tradition, fairy tales, and coffee-cup-theology has taught us that the wolves in sheep's clothing represents wolves appearing as sheep. But according to Ezekiel 34 the "sheep's clothing" isn't referring to wolves trying to look like sheep. It describes the false prophets leading God's flock as pretentious shepherds.

"Son of man, prophesy against the shepherds of Israel... Thus says the Lord God to the shepherds...You... clothe yourselves with the wool..." (Ezekiel 34:2,3).

The shepherds were always clothed with the sheep's wool because it was one of the benefits of shepherding. All leaders within the Church, whether they are true or false, are called shepherds. With that in mind, we need to understand that Jesus is giving us a teaching which helps us discern and expose the false ones.

"Beware of false prophets... inwardly they are ravenous wolves" (Matthew 7:15).

Ravenous Leaders

Ravenous wolves characterizes leaders who are hungry for flesh. I, as a Charismatic preacher, was one of those carnivorous leaders; therefore, I know how this concept can easily be applied to leaders. I know what motivates them. I know what it means to (metaphorically) devour flesh.

The flesh is the opposite of true spiritual understanding. It is the biblical picture of thriving on error. Mind you, I was not aware that my fleshly appetite was wrong, because error had successfully displaced truth in my life and was therefore treated as truth.

The flesh is an attitude in the soul which eventually manifests or ends up being a captivating realm of false concepts. False prophets use false concepts to entice the sheep out of true spiritual safety, which automatically exposes them to the wild beasts of the field. Of course, the irony of this intensifies as we realize that the wild beasts of the field are the carnivorous leaders of God's people – the very leaders who were supposed to protect them.

These wolf-like leaders love to get the Church out of the spirit (protection) and into false experiences and new doctrines (vulnerability). They may even do it by confessing just the opposite, "You must let go, get out of the flesh, and into the Spirit."

Wolves are Natural Carnivores

The wolves do this by instinct and are not even aware that what they are doing could be wrong. After all, they are carnivores. Devouring flesh comes naturally to them.
Wolves cannot be satisfied with a good spiritual meal from the Word of God by itself – they are compelled to feast on an admixture of flesh.

Chapter Six

Limiting their ministry to the revelation of Christ really does not satisfy them. There are many leaders in the Body of Christ who fit this description and Jesus gives us the means to discern them. Christ's teaching is the fortified wall that is made available for our protection against their false doctrines.

The Fruit of Emptiness

"Beware of false prophets, who come to you in sheep's clothing, but inwardly they are ravenous wolves. You will know them by their fruits. Do men gather grapes from thornbushes or figs from thistles? Even so, every good tree bears good fruit, but a bad tree bears bad fruit. A good tree cannot bear bad fruit, nor can a bad tree bear good fruit. Every tree that does not bear good fruit is cut down and thrown into the fire" (Matthew 7:15-20).

There is a very interesting question embedded within these verses. Jesus asked his disciples, "Do men gather grapes from thorns, or figs from thistles?" I asked myself the same question. "What kind of fruit grows on a thorn bush?" I asked the same question about the fruit which comes from thistles. "What kind of fruit grows there?" The answer to both questions is: "NOTHING." We can expand the idea of *nothing* to include what I learned in my study of "false" as useless fruit and emptiness.

Therefore, based on two main points found here and the fact that Jesus went on into the subject of the fruit of the lips in Matthew chapter twelve, we can see what Jesus was teaching us about wolves in sheep's clothing. The revealing fruit of the false prophet isn't signs and wonders, miracles, or crowds of people. The fruit to look for is the emptiness in their preaching, the fruit of their lips, and the common characteristic of wolves – their carnal appetite.

Some people see the signs and wonders in the false prophet's active ministries of today and say, "Look at the fruit."

But if signs and wonders, soulish experiences, and crowds of people were the fruit of true leaders then Jesus wouldn't have said, "*Many* will say to Me in that day, 'Lord, Lord, have we not prophesied in Your name, cast out demons in Your name, and done many wonders in Your name?' And then I will declare to them, 'I never knew you; depart from Me, you who practice lawlessness" (Matthew 7:22,23).

Jesus was showing us the key to discerning false teachers. We are to notice the empty fruit of their lips. In other words, we are to notice the content of their words. Their empty words will expose their lack of fruit.

"For a tree is known by its fruit... How can you, being evil, speak good things? For out of the abundance of the heart the mouth speaks" (Matthew 12:33,34).

An Abundance of Inner Emptiness

The fruit of the false prophet isn't blatant, evil, black lies. The empty fruit of their lips is merely a lack of truth in what they teach. It seems to me that we've been looking for the wrong fruit in order to identify false leaders. Before I saw what this Scripture was saying, I thought I was to discern a false prophet by their visible, ugly fruit. The fact is it's very easy to discern outright lies about God. It's not the blatant or the conspicuous which indicates the fruit of the false prophets within the Church. Why would we need discernment for something obvious? Discernment is needed for something more subtle – to pierce through and expose the abundance of words which sound spiritual but are void of the Gospel of Christ. We need to discern preaching in which the truth is mysteriously missing.

These wolf-like leaders sound like preachers, look like preachers, but the true Gospel message is not a vital part of their main teaching.

Chapter Six

When considering the fruit of the false prophet and his false signs and wonders, we must understand what we are looking for. Jesus said we could test their fruit. Yet there seems to be many ideas of what that test should be. The testing of the spirits according to 1 John chapter four, seems to be the least understood.

Test 1
"But Look at the Changed Lives"

I've heard of many tests which are used by Christians. In defending some strange manifestations, well meaning Christians have pointed to the fact that many people claim their lives are "changed." But claiming transformed lives isn't true fruit. New-Age cults and self-improvement groups all testify of changed lives. Many people involved in religion claim their lives are dramatically altered for the better. There is an abundance of false experiences and emotional affirmations available to them. They will confess they are happier, are more fulfilled, and are set free in many areas of their lives. So, the fruit of "changed lives" still leaves room for more testing.

Test 2
"But, They Love Jesus"

I've heard people claim that after they experienced a strange manifestation, they became more in "love with Jesus" than ever before. This isn't true fruit either because there are many concepts of Jesus out there. Not all who name the name of Christ are actually following a biblical image of Him.

Paul warned us to be careful not to follow a different Jesus, a different spirit, or a different Gospel (2 Corinthians 11:4). Even Jesus Himself said that there would be *many* false Christs.

TEST 3
"BUT LOOK AT THE CROWDS"

We often approve of ministries because of their apparent success and popular acceptance. But crowds of people, success, and popularity are not true Christ-like fruit either. Even if leaders endorse and approve of each other's ministries for the benefit of wary believers, we need to be aware that there is still room for testing.

THE BEST TEST

True, godly, Christ-like fruit is revealed when the words of leaders, the spiritual results, and manifestations of their ministries completely agree with what Jesus said and did in the flesh. The only way we are going to discern the false is by studying and understanding everything that Jesus represented in the flesh.

FALSE PROPHETS AMONG YOU

Some results which are often mistaken for good fruit are supernatural visions and dreams. People assume that if something supernatural happens to them, God is moving in their lives. I know by experience that people naturally followed my "flakey" prophecies more than they followed my good basic Bible teachings. Giving them a "mixture" of holy and unholy was the worst thing I could do as a pastor. Many of my visions and dreams lacked agreement with Scripture; but we followed them anyway.

JESUS IS THE TEST

If you wanted to make a list of all true, godly manifestations and miracles and wanted to know where they were listed, they could all be found in Jesus' earthly ministry. Furthermore, all of the manifestations in Jesus' ministry can also be found in the Old Testament. Not one miracle performed by Jesus was invented on the spot. Therefore, if we witness a spiritual manifestation not found in Jesus' earthly ministry, you can be very sure that it is extra-biblical and you would be right to test it. This is why, in the ministry of discernment, the knowledge of the Word is so important. Only ignorance will keep us from discerning the false. The truth about any subject can be found in the Bible. All Bible subjects and parables are made alive in Jesus' life. We have not been left without the true source of discernment that we so desperately need.

Laziness in the Church has become the real enemy of discernment. People get involved in false manifestations because they want a shortcut to freedom without taking the time to steadfastly continue in the Word of God.

Jesus said, "*continue* in my Word and you shall know the truth and the truth will set you free." But our microwave society mindset cannot grasp that true freedom in the kingdom of God is progressive. Why should we continue in the Word when we think we can just flock to a wild meeting and get all the freedom we want instantly and effortlessly?

INSTANT GRATIFICATION

We are being seduced into instant gratification of the flesh. We're no longer living in a long-term covenant relationship with Christ.

Our marriage to Him is no longer a two-way relationship but a one-way, selfish convenience. We have been led away from the essence of the new covenant.

Our understanding of faith in God is being twisted into a "candyman" mentality. The sweet sensation of healing has become our goal instead of seeking to know the Healer. When we keep going in this direction, we open up to false signs and wonders because we remain caught in the sense realm instead of developing the faith of the inner man by feeding on the Word.

We've become lovers of self instead of lovers of God; therefore, we follow anyone who will fluff us up. But, if any preacher challenges us for more commitment, we scream "condemnation."

Our discernment needs to be developed beyond the realm of our feelings. True discernment comes through the knowledge of God and His Word. It does not come through soulish sensations. If we think discernment is based on our feelings, we will remain trapped in the flesh.

My Soulish Sensations

The Devil is the master of the carnal soul. The carnal soul, in my estimation, is a soul governed by the flesh and not by the spirit. The Devil loves to play with the feelings of the soul and trick people into thinking they're walking in the spirit.

In my own life, my sensations in the flesh became synonymous, in my mind, with being led by the Spirit. The trap was set and my fleshly ideas began to displace the true inspiration of the Holy Spirit.

The reason this worked was because truth was either belittled or long forgotten. The sense realm took precedence over the knowledge of the truth and sensations, experiences, and feelings were exalted as spiritual.

This strategy has worked in the Church because the knowledge of the Word has been portrayed as boring and dry by preachers who use disrespectful innuendoes like "Word hard" and "theology." Some preachers have made those who study the Word look like they're "heady" and not open to the Spirit. As a result, the Church has become embittered with biblical knowledge. The Word of God is placed on the shelf and wild meetings become more important than quiet evenings in the Word.

MANY WILL SAY I AM CHRIST

"For many will come in my name, saying, 'I am the Christ,' and will deceive many..." (Matthew 24:5).

We need to understand what Jesus is saying here. We can make these few words mean two different things. It all hinges on where we place the quotations marks or how we read it.

If we interpret this to mean we are to watch out for those who would say of themselves, "I am Christ," then this verse will apply to only a few people. We will then place this warning far from the reach of our own hearts.

But if we read it without the quotation marks, it takes on a whole new meaning. We are to be aware that even though a person can declare or confess with their lips that Jesus is the Christ, it also means that same person can deceive us.

If you think about this verse in this way, then it applies to all Christians, and in particular, to Christian leaders. We all come in His name, we all declare that He is the Christ; but it also means that if we do not heed the warning, we can either be deceived or deceive others. You see, the problem is more subtle and harder to discern than we first thought.

This is the unpleasant part of my testimony. I was a dangerous leader to follow because I came in Jesus' name, I zealously preached that Jesus was the Christ, but I also led many people into confusion and deception.

PSEUDO-CHRIST

"False prophets will rise..." (Matthew 24:24).
The word for "false" comes from the Greek word "pseudo."

The meaning of this word portrays the idea of something which isn't real, something counterfeit, a falsehood, a lie, or a deception. We use pseudo in our everyday language to convey the concepts of false, bogus, and phony.

From this brief overview and with a little biblical study of false prophets, we can easily conclude that a false prophet is a pseudo prophet who speaks a counterfeit spiritual message and portrays a pseudo-image of Christ.

They may not be genuine godly leaders within the body of Christ, nonetheless, they are recognized as leaders within the setting of the Christian Church.

Leaders under the influence of antichrist spirits lead people into wrong doctrines and wrong attitudes. Some false leaders may be aware of this while others may not. But the result of following their teachings will still be the same.

The Bible shows us this through simple parabolic language – false shepherds lead a flock of sheep astray through false teachings. Through these words, "deception, seduction, and lead astray," the Bible paints a picture of sheep who are led astray and scattered on the mountains without proper leaders. When they are alone on the mountains or in the wilderness, they are left to themselves and eat anything they find. They are exposed to the wild, carnivorous beasts of the field. This is symbolic of the dangers of little ones who follow false teachings.

When the disciples asked Jesus about the signs of the last days, the first thing He mentioned was deception. He told them to "take heed." This means "to watch out, beware, keep your eyes peeled, and don't be so naive." Why? False christs are going to make their way into leadership and high places of honor among God's people. And they are not coming to aid the Church into a deeper understanding of Jesus. They are coming into the fold to deceive the elect and lead them into false concepts of Christ.

Chapter Six

We must understand that the Devil wants to be seen as more like Christ than he wants to be seen unlike Him. He doesn't want to be exposed as the destroyer. He wants to be known as the god of amazing signs and wonders.

"For false christs and false prophets will rise and show great signs and wonders to deceive, if possible, even the elect" (Matthew 24:24).

"And Jesus answered and said to them: 'Take heed that no one deceives you'" (Matthew 24:4).

WATCH OUT!

If the Word of God tells us to take heed and to beware in the last days then why don't we do it? Why do we go on as if this Scripture doesn't apply to us? We seem to think that the leaders will do it for us. But the leaders, in many cases, lack discernment. In fact, in some cases, the leaders are the ones who approve of false teachings.

Why don't we test our doctrines and beliefs? Why are these Scriptures in the Bible? Are we to ignore them and assume that we, of all people, cannot be deceived?

No, it's time to sharpen up the Sword of the Spirit – the revelation of Jesus Christ – and be on guard. It would be better for us to be on guard than to remain ignorant of God's Living Word.

"See, I have told you beforehand" (Matthew 24:25).

Jesus didn't say there would be just a few deceivers in the last days. He said there would be *many*. "For *many* shall come... and shall deceive *many*." This indicates that deception in the latter times is going to be common. There won't be just a few isolated cases. It will be all around us.

"*Many* will say to Me in that day, 'Lord, Lord, have we not prophesied in Your name, cast out demons in Your name, and done many wonders in Your name?' And then I will declare to them, 'I never knew you; depart from Me, you who practice lawlessness'!" (Matthew 7:22-23).

"And *many* will follow (false teachers and) their destructive ways..." (2 Peter 2:2).

"Even now *many* antichrists have come" (1 John 2:18).

"Because *many* false prophets have gone out into the world" (1 John 4:1).

"For *many* deceivers have gone out into the world who do not confess Jesus Christ as coming in the flesh. This is a deceiver and an antichrist" (2 John 1:7).

◆ Chapter Seven

SUBMISSION TO LEADERSHIP

We are all hungry for more of God. But without leaders, who will lead us into the right pastures? We may end up eating in pastures which are not good for us. The fact that we are hungry is not a point against submitted sheep, but throughout Scripture, God deals with a heavy hand with leaders who take advantage of the hunger in God's people.

The Devil is very skilled and accomplished at handling the Word of God deceitfully. Using the hunger in God's people to his advantage is one of his specialties.

The fact that I was led into deception for many years was not because I had a black heart. Since my salvation in 1970, I have been hungry for God. That hunger has been the compelling force which has caused me to jump onto almost every new-doctrine bandwagon that has swept through the Spirit-filled Church.

I agree with you if you say, "This is truly a sign of immaturity," but without true leaders who will nurture us in the knowledge of the stature of Christ, we are easily tossed to and fro by every new wind of teaching. In fact, it is a shame, but leaders within the Church are the ones who have often introduced us to many new winds of doctrine.

As I look back at my younger years in my home church, I realize that my pastors (and there was a series of them) did not publicly correct the foolishness that took place in our church. Why that was, I can only speculate. I would guess that it was because they did not discern the problems in the first place. I cannot accept the idea that my pastors actually knew right from wrong and kept it to themselves. I choose to believe they gave me all they could.

However, this brings us to very important question. Where does the buck stop? Which level of leadership must face the responsibility for the condition of the food (teaching) which was given to the sheep in God's pasture?

I suppose that most pastors would prefer to pass the buck to a level of leadership above them. I would venture to guess that leaders of the next level would blame their colleges, their professors, their spiritual mentors, and even their church founders. The sobering reality of all this is; leaders, no matter what level they are at, are destined to face a heavier hand, than those submitted sheep who sit under their teaching. We can discern this by looking at how Jesus rebuked the Pharisees and other leaders of Israel. We can then compare that to how Jesus handled the ordinary man on the street. I get the impression that God does use a heavier hand with any leader who places himself at the head of the class.

"My brethren, let not many of you become teachers, knowing that we shall receive a stricter judgment" (James 3:1).

SUBMISSION AT ALL COSTS

When I, as a leader, participated in various winds of doctrine, I did it with the attitude of "submitting" under the present day leaders of the Church. "Submission" has always been a

Chapter Seven

strong part of my Christian walk. Therefore, I worked hard at finding spiritual leaders I could appreciate and submitted myself under their teachings.

When I became a pastor, I continued to find ministries, movements, and leaders under whom I could submit myself and my church. It had become a hard and fast rule in our Charismatic camp to have some type of covering. We never enjoyed being labeled "independent" or "out there on their own."

Even in recent years, as I have uncovered many false doctrines in my own ministry and shared them with other ministers, they would accuse me of being deceived. In the minds of my peers, I now disagreed with and would not submit under the accepted spiritual leaders of our day – especially if any doctrine I challenged was still widely accepted and taught by "men of renown."

As a Charismatic minister, I submitted myself and my church under a well-known Canadian pastor along with his associates and contacts. I earned a place on the front row at their major camp-meetings with the rest of the faithful. I liked the attention, the cameras, the lights, and the action. If we were encouraged to "yell at the Devil," I would yell the loudest. If we were to praise the Lord and "dance all night," I would dance the hardest. We were up front where all the action was. Not only were we finally able to see and experience things firsthand, but we were at the center of attention. Several times, the pastor acknowledged me by name in front of my peers. I enjoyed the long awaited honor of being received into the "inner circle."

I Was Alarmed

During this time of "submission," I continued to search my own heart and spent much time in the scriptures trying to understand the revelation of Christ and how it exposed the false.

Slowly my understanding was being opened and I could see things I hadn't seen before. My discernment was growing and I began to be alarmed with the vision and direction of the camp and the spiritual leadership I was following.

It was a turbulent time for me. I was beginning to see what was happening around me while at the same time, I was trying even harder to submit. Submission was more important to me than exposing false ideas. Therefore, when they called us by name to the platform to receive a fresh dose of "laughing in the spirit," and some of the other "extra-biblical" blessing, I quickly moved to where the action was and did my best to go with the flow. I was frustrated because my biblical studies were telling me that these popular manifestations were false. At the same time, I did not want to appear "rebellious," so I did my best to yield. After all, if I could "see," surely my peers and my leaders would confirm it because they were more respected, anointed, and sensitive to the Spirit than I was.

It just grew more agonizing to submit and keep the knowledge of what was true and what was false hidden in my own heart. I decided to quietly "slip out" of the movement and had the unpleasant task of telling my own church of my decision.

What a wonderful group of people they were! Even in the midst of belonging to one of the most popular movements in the Charismatic Church, they graciously followed me in this decision.

We, as a church, have never turned back. The revelation of Christ, coupled with the understanding of the false, has set us free. And the freedom and the reward of Christ have been more than enough compensation for the "loneliness" of transition.

Fear of Men

During this time, one of the most challenging and disturbing things I had to deal with was the fear of men. Since we were

Chapter Seven

taught to submit and I was beginning to rebel and challenge the teachings of respected leaders, the result was predictable. The camp I was a part of, gave me the silent treatment. Only a few challenged me over my new doctrinal position. Some of my best friends, though, began to openly rebuke me or target me from the pulpit. If you are a "people person" like I am, this can be very effective. In fact, the same tactic is still used today. But, since I've dealt with it, and have come to understand how it works, I've replaced the fear of rejection of men with a healthy fear and respect for the Lord.

◆ Chapter Eight

NEW DOCTRINES AND MOVEMENTS

In recent years, we have noticed a rise in interest in revival centers. Usually, these are churches and ministries scattered throughout the world where something "different" is taking place. These special places are supposed to house a "sovereign move of God" of refreshing and revival. Christians sense that they need to get to one of these special meetings where they believe there is a specific anointing or blessing that can be found nowhere else. Their mentality is this: "if we travel to that meeting, we will be refreshed and our lives will be changed." So they drive by car, hop on a bus, or travel by air to a revival center in Toronto, Pensacola, England, or Sweden to have a life-changing experience.

If only the Christian life was that simple. All we would have to do is travel to the latest "Azusa Street" revival and everything would be wonderful. But the Christian life isn't like that. It is not instantaneous: it is progressive.

Several pastors and leaders have asked me, "What do you think of these revival centers such as Toronto or Pensacola?" I've told them that this question cannot be answered with one

Chapter Eight

blanket statement without addressing what happens to the people in these meetings or without questioning each manifestation and experience – one at a time.

Why do we have to take on one manifestation at a time? The reason is simple; many strange, wild, and even demonic manifestations are found in these movements and ministries. It isn't just one simple issue. Many assumptions have to be addressed. Doctrines from our past, which have been handed down to us by our spiritual forefathers, need to be examined. Our own pre-conceived ideas about how God moves needs to be questioned in the light of the revelation of Christ. We need to be willing to re-examine our opinions about which manifestations are of God and which ones are not. Why do people shake to portray the presence of God? Why do people cry, moan, or laugh to prove that the Holy Spirit is doing something supernatural to them? Why do people think they have to fall down when they are touched by the man of God?

WHY DO PEOPLE FALL DOWN?

Where did "falling under the power" come from and who started it? This manifestation was not found in Jesus' ministry, so why do we do it? The reason we have to ask this question is because Jesus was anointed more than any man who will ever live; yet when He prayed for people, they did not fall down nor were they slain in the Spirit. They were physically healed, changed, and the actual results were seen by everyone.

I have fallen "under the power" dozens of times. That is why I can tell you, by experience, that the fear of man and the fear of missing out has always been the strongest reason for most people to fall to the floor. Of course, I did not realize it at the time.

Nevertheless, I eventually came to my senses and saw my true motive: I did not want to look less willing than anyone else.

Nor did I want my "inability to yield" to the "moving of the Spirit" to be interpreted as rebellion or unbelief.

When you are standing in front of all your peers with respected leaders available to minister to you and they lay their hands on you, the pressure is on – especially when you are up on stage and all expectant eyes are watching you. That is why many preachers have followed this pattern. They find more success with "manifestations" if they call miracle candidates up to the platform. The intimidation of the platform "weeds out" those who are uncertain and draws out those who are more open to new manifestations.

I can tell you by experience that it wasn't the fear of God I was struggling with: It was the fear of not looking as spiritual as some of the others. Fear causes us to go with the flow even if it doesn't make sense.

I Was Pretending

As time went on, I got quite good at pretending when I was "hit by the anointing." At one time in particular, I was hungry for a move of God in my life. I went forward for ministry at a camp-meeting. I was so deceived by this time that I actually believed falling down was the same as a "work of God" in my life.

The floor of the old chapel was uncarpeted, cold, bare concrete. I went forward to receive what the preacher had to impart. It was typical of many meetings I had attended over the years. There were appointed ushers standing behind those receiving prayer to "catch" them as they fell backwards to the floor. The preacher laid his hands upon me, and I immediately "yielded" and fell backwards according to my Pentecostal traditions. In the middle of my descent to the cold hard concrete floor, I realized there wasn't a "catcher" behind me and in midair, I could

Chapter Eight

hear the entire congregation "gasp" in unity. I'm sure the building lost air pressure for a second. My tall frame hit the concrete with a thud. I lay there in astonishment and wondered what I should do. I was so used to playing the game by that time that I just lay there and pretended that God was doing a work in my life. I did not do this to deceive the people. It was my Charismatic theology which led me to believe that pretending was the same as faith.

For many years as a pastor, I watched people fall to the floor when I laid hands on them. The preachers and the people were well trained in this, and we all knew what was expected of each other. We had quickly caught on to the traditions of the Charismatic Church.

DID JESUS DO IT?

Did Jesus cause people to fall under the power in His ministry? Did He see people laugh, bark, and roll as they received their healing? Did Jesus' anointing overcome them and send them flying? Did they fall down and shake or cry as He laid hands on them? Only the demon possessed manifested such foolishness and Jesus usually told them to be quiet. He did not accept these manifestations as a normal part of His ministry.

Why have we accepted this kind of thing as from God? I believe that we have made traditions out of wrong spiritual manifestations. We need to repent and turn back to Jesus as our standard for what we believe. We need to cast down the high esteem we hold for "Azusa Street" and other revivals. We need to see them as gatherings of immature people who were eagerly seeking God, but were easily misled. We can learn from them but we do not have to idolize them.

Jesus was anointed in greater capacity than any man of God alive today. No preacher can boast that they are doing or teaching anything different than Christ and still be right in their doctrine. If they are constantly seeing different miracles in their ministry than those seen in Jesus' earthly ministry, they had better start asking some questions.

SLAIN IN THE SPIRIT

Who invented the phrase "slain in the Spirit?" We need to take a closer look at the Scriptures we have used to substantiate this doctrine.

First of all, let's make it clear that biblical references to "falling on their face" before God, kings, rulers, and angels are very common in the Bible. Just because these people bowed their faces to the ground and gave honor does not mean that the Spirit of God made them do it. There are more than forty references in the Bible to "falling on their faces" as a gesture of honor and there are more than twenty that refer to "bowing down to the ground." None of the references suggested that people were struck down or forced to the floor by God.

In the Pentecostal and Charismatic Church movements to which I have belonged, two of the most popular Scriptures used to herald this doctrine are from two identical passages:

"So that the priests could not stand to minister by reason of the cloud: for the glory of the LORD had filled the house of God" (2 Chronicles 5:14, KJV).

"So that the priests could not stand to minister because of the cloud: for the glory of the LORD had filled the house of the LORD" (1 Kings 8:11, KJV)

The theory is that the priests "fell down" because of the "glory cloud." But this doctrine is based on an assumption which is easily exposed by the context which also states:

"And it came to pass, when the priests *came out* of the holy place, that the cloud filled the house of the Lord" (1 Kings 8:10).

Chapter Eight

"And it came to pass when the priests *came out* of the Most Holy Place..." (2 Chronicles 5:11).

How could the priests be "slain" by the "glory cloud" that filled the temple if they were no longer in the temple? A more accurate interpretation suggests that the priests could not "stand" or return to their place to minister because the glory of God had filled the place where they were to stand. It does not mean that they were flat on their backs unable to move. It simply means that the priests had to stand outside the temple with the rest of the people who were awed by the spectacle.

One Scripture, which paints a clearer picture of what actually happened, is found in 2 Chronicles 7:1-2.

"When Solomon had finished praying, fire came down from Heaven and consumed the burnt offering and the sacrifices; and the glory of the Lord filled the temple. And the priests could not enter the house of the Lord, because the glory of the Lord had filled the Lord's house" (2 Chronicles 7:1-2).

OH, THE GLORY CLOUD

The other assumption heard throughout Charismatic circles is that the glory and the cloud are the same thing. I have witnessed countless times when preachers declared, "Oh, the glory cloud has just entered the building and it is now billowing from the back of the church to the front!"

In actuality, in the Bible, the glory of God was indeed the manifest presence of God Himself. But the cloud was not the glory. It was the shield or the veil which separated the glory of God from man. Not only did it protect unholy man from being exposed directly to the holiness of God, but the true image of God was hidden behind the cloud.

This is the cloud that was removed when Jesus came to the earth. He revealed the glory of God to us so we would never have to "look" through cloud cover again. This speaks of the tremendous unhindered clarity of the character of God that He brought to us.

Jesus is the manifest presence of God to man. The manifest presence of God, which so many are searching for, is not a sensation in a meeting or a vision of the "glory cloud." To suggest the need for an Old Testament manifestation of the glory cloud of God's presence contradicts the sufficiency of the New Testament revelation of Christ.

RAISED UP BY THE SPIRIT

The other fact that we need to consider is whenever the prophets and apostles were exposed to the revelation of God's presence, they were not allowed to remain prostrate on the ground. They were repeatedly raised up and strengthened by the Spirit of God to receive God's instructions. Now this seems to be exactly opposite to our modern day interpretations of what happens when God reveals Himself. I've always assumed that if God manifested Himself to me I would not be able to get up off the floor. But many Old Testament prophets were commanded to *stand up* in God's holy presence.

This happened to Ezekiel.

"The appearance of the likeness of the glory of the Lord. So when I saw it, I fell on my face, and I heard a voice of One speaking. And He said to me, "Son of man, *stand on your feet*, and I will speak to you." Then the Spirit entered me when He spoke to me, and set me on my feet; and I heard Him who spoke to me" (Ezekiel 1:28 - 2:2).

"The glory of the Lord stood there, like the glory which I saw by the River Chebar; and I fell on my face. Then the Spirit entered me and *set me on my feet*..." (Ezekiel 3:23,24).

It also happened to the prophet Daniel.

Chapter Eight

"When he came I was afraid and fell on my face... but he touched me, and *stood me upright*" (Daniel 8:17).

It also happened to the Apostle Paul.

"Then he fell to the ground, and heard a voice saying to him... So he, trembling and astonished, said, "Lord, what do You want me to do?" Then the Lord said to him, "*Arise* and go into the city, and you will be told what you must do" (Acts 9:4-6).

A similar thing happened to the Apostle John.

"And when I saw Him, I fell at His feet as dead. But He laid His right hand on me, saying... *Write* the things which you have seen..." (Revelation 1:17).

Since sharing this understanding with friends, we have had some fun with the idea of perhaps laying on the floor until the "anointed man of God" lays his hands upon us to raise us to our feet. Now, that would be something to see! Yes, it sounds like an impressive idea, but I'm sure you understand that this is a humorous poke at what happens in prayer lines across the country. It still disagrees with Jesus' earthly ministry.

My point is this: it is more scriptural to be raised up to obey God than it is to fall down. Instead of falling down as a sign of God's anointing, maybe we should just simply be willing to grow in the knowledge of Christ until God raises us up to preach the Gospel.

DELIVERANCE GONE TOO FAR

Another issue which needs to be addressed is the "sovereign deliverance" of unsuspecting candidates at these special meetings. We have to ask the question, "Did Jesus cast out devils out of people who were not willing to be free or from those who were not aware of their needs?

The demoniac who was possessed with a legion of demons came and worshipped at Jesus' feet just before Jesus set him free. It is interesting to note that those demons, even though they were a legion, could not stop the man from coming to Jesus. Perhaps the Devil does not control our choices as much as we have imagined!

These questions we are asking about deliverance are really addressing what we think about how God deals with bondage. Does God "deliver" unsuspecting candidates?

We must always remember that Jesus Christ is the express image of God and the standard for all truth. He is the pattern for ministry and He can help us understand God's methods of deliverance. He fully revealed God's true character and God's true methods of ministry to us. There isn't one vital thing, not one act of God, missing from Jesus' earthly ministry.

If these revival manifestations of shaking, rolling, and growling are the result of deliverance through which the true character of God is being revealed, then let us all participate. But, if these manifestations do not agree with the character of God revealed in Christ, then we have every right to question, discern, and – if need be – dismiss them as false.

A Big Surprise

If there is such a thing as a surprise "move of God," then we should see evidence of it in Jesus' earthly ministry. Did Jesus bypass the will of man to pour out miracles upon them? Through Jesus, was God revealed as a God who was in complete control of people's experiences? Did He show Himself fully through the revelation of Christ or just partially?

If Jesus was the express image of God, then we have to ask these questions: Did Jesus pick and choose who would be saved, healed, delivered or not? Was the unbelief of Nazareth planned by God? Did Jerusalem reject Jesus because God willed it? Did Jesus control the spiritual environment around Him? If He did,

Chapter Eight

then what we have assumed about a move of God is true; but if He did not, then we may have to change our doctrines.

A Few Assumptions

We have to deal with a few assumptions concerning the characteristics that have been commonly attributed to the Godhead. Here are a few examples:

1. God the Father's ministry was specific to the Old Testament.

2. Jesus had His own brand of ministry on the earth, which was different than His Father's.

3. The Holy Spirit has different manifestations in His present day ministry than what was seen in Jesus' earthly ministry.

All of these examples suggest that God the Father, God the Son, and God the Holy Spirit have three individual characters, agendas, and ministries. Doctrines which are not founded on the revelation of Christ bring us to these conclusions.

By observing Jesus as our ultimate standard for truth we can safely conclude the following: God is not controlling our environments; He will never bypass anyone's will; He will never bust in and change a person without their own personal faith in Jesus Christ. God is all powerful and willing to work on our behalf, and that power is available to every person who has faith. But, faith cannot be activated properly without understanding the true character of God as revealed through His Son.

What we must understand is that God the Father, God the Son, and God the Holy Spirit walk in absolute agreement. They were all revealed perfectly through Jesus' earthly ministry.

"How God anointed Jesus of Nazareth with the Holy Spirit and with power, who went about doing good and healing all who were oppressed by the devil, for God was with Him" (Acts 10:38).

Right Under Your Nose

Even Philip, one of the disciples who followed and watched Jesus for several years, still had trouble understanding the true character of the Father.

"Philip said to Him, "Lord, show us the Father, and it is sufficient for us. Jesus said to him, 'Have I been with you so long, and yet you have not known Me, Philip? He who has seen Me has seen the Father; so how can you say, 'Show us the Father'?" (John 14:8,9).

What Jesus was saying was, "Philip, every time I laid hands on the sick I showed you the Father. Every time I cast out a devil, I showed you the Father. Every time I rebuked the Pharisees, I showed you the Father and after all this time, are you still asking me to show you the Father?" He said, "I am the way, the truth, and the life." This means that He was the way to God; but it also means that He revealed to us the ways of God – all of them. He was the truth about God and the life of God revealed in living color.

I have heard many people confess, "I want to know the ways of God." Well, that's a very noble thing to say, but the solution is very simple – almost too simple. If we want to know God, we have to look at Jesus!

Jesus said to him, "I am the way, the truth, and the life. No one comes to the Father except through Me. If you had known Me, you would have known My Father also; and from now on you know Him and have seen Him" (John 14:6-7).

Jesus sought out those who would hear Him and walked away from those who would not. This revealed the Father. He healed those who would receive, but did not sovereignly pick and choose who would be healed. This revealed the Father. He did not force healing on the unwilling, but looked for faith and obedience. When those ingredients were found, there were

Chapter Eight

miracles. This revealed the Father.

As He represented the Father, Jesus never said "No" to those who came seeking Him with the right heart, and yet, He never bypassed their will and sovereignly pushed healing onto them either. He never healed or delivered anyone without them either coming to Him by faith or by obeying His commands. If He told them to take up their bed and walk and they obeyed Him, even by showing the slightest bit of effort, there was a miracle. If they didn't come by faith, but only came because they were seeking proof through signs and wonders, they weren't provided any. If they did not obey Jesus' words, then nothing took place. In all of this, He was revealing the truth about His Father.

LET THEM WALK AWAY

Not everyone received the blessings that Jesus wanted to impart. For instance, He was willing for the rich young ruler to follow Him and be blessed, but the rich young ruler rejected the opportunity and walked away (Matthew 19:16-26).

Jesus didn't chase after him or try to convince him to make the right choice. Jesus did not call him back and say, "You don't understand, I am the Son of God! Here, I will show you a miracle to prove it! Watch Me heal this person! Let Me prove to you who I am before you walk away!" No, Jesus did not do that. He honored the man's decision and let the man choose his own way. There is no one else who has revealed the ways of God more accurately than Jesus!

WHERE DID SPIRITUAL WARFARE COME FROM?

We as a Church became actively involved in a hyper brand of spiritual warfare. We would pray for hours at a time trying to change the spiritual climate of our community and our nation. We did not just pray once a week or when it was convenient. We prayed together as a church every weekday morning from 7:00 a.m. to 8:00 a.m. and, during that time of intense prayer, we believed that we were waging a spiritual war that had to be won via strong, loud, committed prayer.

It was a very real battle for us at the time. I began to question this practice when I was studying the biblical use of the word "false." I was also strongly convicted by the life of Jesus. He did not wage this kind of spiritual warfare nor did He teach it. Over the years, my entire view on spiritual warfare has dramatically changed, and I want to share my findings.

A False Concept of God

Much of today's spiritual warfare teaching stems from a false concept of God. Typically, a false concept of God will usually result in a false concept of prayer. I have discovered that whatever our image of God is, it directly influences the type of Christian we will try to be. Usually, the results of how we think will be most evident in our prayer life.

If God is a bully with a big stick, we will try to bully people in our prayer life. If God orchestrates life's miseries, then Christians will believe in praying precatory prayers. If God overlooks unbridled living, then our prayer life will reflect an unhealthy tolerance of sin and rebellion. If God gives away expensive cars and big screen TVs to whomever asks Him, then our prayers will be occupied with the riches of this world. If we think God will bypass the will of men and bless them or humble them without their consent, then our prayer life will reflect the same degree of control. Whatever concept of God to which we hold, will determine what kind of prayers we will pray.

Chapter Eight

JESUS IS THE TRUE CONCEPT OF GOD

Jesus was willing for the people of Nazareth to receive Him in order to bring them the deliverance and the healing to which they were entitled. However, they didn't believe in Him and tried to push Him over a cliff. There was great resistance to the Gospel in Nazareth, but Jesus didn't do spiritual warfare over the city. He didn't try to further convince the unbelieving people through signs and wonders. Jesus didn't try to push His doctrine on them or attempt to prove to them who He was, before He moved on. He just went to the next town and preached the Gospel of the Kingdom there.

I've talked to some preachers who think that Jesus made a big mistake in how He handled His hometown. They reason that Jesus was immature in His ministry and was too abrasive in His hometown. They hint that Jesus changed his tactics after Nazareth. They don't realize it but they are condemning Jesus for what happened at Nazareth.

Jesus never made any mistakes! The Bible says that Jesus fully pleased the Father and did the will of God completely. He was perfectly right in how He handled places like Nazareth and Jerusalem. If the Father were to handle the same situations on His own, then He would have done exactly the same as His Son.

Jesus stood over the city of Jerusalem and cried because they wouldn't recognize their time of visitation. The Messiah had come to its streets and had found only a few who would receive healing and deliverance through Him.

I can almost hear spiritual warfare preachers saying, "Jesus, what are you crying about? Get down there and do some miracles. We can take this city! Let's show them God's power! Let's pull down the Devil's stronghold from over this place! As soon as we cast down the strongman of this city, their eyes will be opened and they will receive you. They will flock to you by the thousands. Come on Jesus don't give up so easily. We can take back what the Devil has stolen!"

Christian Political Activism

It's not just our prayer life that has been affected with this kind of thinking. The Church's "political activism" comes from the same misunderstanding. We seem to forget that Jesus did not come to change the Roman Empire. He did not come to the earth to change the political views of the Jews. He came to establish a kingdom not of this world.

For some reason, we are so busy trying to change the world around us, that we forget our true position here on the earth. We are foreigners here. The Church is likened to an embassy in a strange land, and we are but ambassadors for Christ on foreign soil. If we would consider the role of an embassy in another part of the world, we would recognize that the embassy does not dictate new laws and standards to its host country. The embassy remains independent and stays out of the affairs of the country in which it is situated and continues there only as a mere guest. The embassy is positioned there for the sake of its own citizens and for those who want to emigrate.

It is a similar situation for the Church. We belong to another kingdom, a kingdom not of this world. We are to pattern ourselves after the King of kings who, when he walked this earth, showed very little interest in the kings of this world. Even King Herod could not ruffle Jesus' purpose. Only when this political leader tried to stop His ministry did Jesus reply, "Go tell that fox...."

Our prayer life can reflect a wrong image of Jesus when we pray for our nations, our cities, and our neighbors. We seem to think that God will sovereignly break into their mundane lives

Chapter Eight

with a "wake up call" while we keep silent. I think we forget God isn't our servant, we are His.

The only way we are going to see our nations change is to preach the Gospel to them, one individual at a time. Even then, we may end up with the same results as Jesus. A handful of disciples followed Him while the majority of Israel did not.

DID JESUS DO ENOUGH?

"Warfare" kind of thinking opposes the revelation of Christ simply because it suggests that Jesus didn't do all that could be done to perform the will of God. It implies that Jesus didn't take it far enough. It leads us to believe we can do things that He could not do. This kind of thinking needs to be challenged. How can Jesus be our example as the first-born of God, the preeminent one, and our flawless forerunner if we think we can do better? Are we superior to Jesus? Do we have greater anointing than the Son of God or do we have a different ministry than His? We answer "no" with our lips, but we say "yes" with our doctrines and our actions – especially in spiritual warfare thinking.

"Most assuredly, I say to you, a servant is not greater than his master; nor is he who is sent greater than he who sent him" (John 13:16).

"A disciple is not above his teacher, nor a servant above his master" (Matthew 10:24).

Now I realize that we are to be conformed into His image, and our goal is to be like Him. But we will never be greater than the original Son. He has wrought a great victory on the cross to give us the opportunity to become like Him but we will never surpass Him. We are to focus upon His image and, as we do, we will be transformed by what we see in Him from glory to glory, from revelation to revelation, with the help of the Holy Spirit.

Nothing Missing

He is the same yesterday, today, and forever. He was the same on the earth as He is in Heaven. He showed us the total will of God – there wasn't any information about God missing from His doctrine. He did not overlook one detail. At the end of His ministry on the earth, He hadn't fallen short of any task. He said to His Father:

"I have glorified You on the earth. I have finished the work which You have given Me to do" (John 17:4).

He fully pleased the Father and fully revealed the Godhead to us in His body. He manifested the very essence of God in His flesh. He was God's true character in concentrated form.

Jesus wasn't just representing the good side of God while He walked the earth. Through Him, the love of God was revealed along with the holiness of God. The mercy of God was revealed along with the judgment of God. He was the entire character of God poured into flesh so we could clearly see Him!

God will not reward those who worship a false concept of Him. He will not answer prayers that are based on wrong ideas or misapplied Scriptures. God will not do a miracle for someone who has a different image of Him than the one revealed in the face of His Son. God doesn't come to those who have a false concept of Him and say, "Oh well, close enough. I guess I will bypass the image of Christ and reward you anyway." God the Father is not – and never will be – anti-Christ.

Does God Have Many Faces?

Two major teachings, which have caused us to be lax on some of these issues are "God has many faces," and "God can manifest Himself to us in any way He pleases." If we have been involved with any religious background at all, these are doctrines with which we may have some difficulty.

First of all, God doesn't have many faces – He only has one: He looks exactly like His Son. He does not manifest Himself in any other way than the way He manifested Himself in Christ.

"For it is the God who commanded light to shine out of darkness, who has shone in our hearts to give the light of the knowledge of the glory of God in the *face* of Jesus Christ" (2 Corinthians 4:6).

"Jesus said to him, "I am the way, the truth, and the life. No one comes to the Father except through Me. If you had known Me, you would have known My Father also; and from now on you know Him and have seen Him" (John 14:6,7).

There is only one true concept of God, and it was revealed in Jesus Christ. There is no other!

We need to repent and turn from all other false, religious concepts and turn back to the living Word of God for guidance. The greatest source of discernment available to us is the Word, which was made alive in the flesh of Christ (Hebrews 4:12, John 1:14).

Is God Going to Rip Evil Out of the Earth?

A false concept of God permeates the Church. This may be the reason for the success of a false prophecy which swept through the Charismatic Church in 1994. A pastor claimed that he had a special prophetic experience in his room one night. He claimed God had said to Him, "I am going to rip evil out of the earth." In order for the prophecy to have been fulfilled, God would have had to bypass the Gospel of Jesus Christ.

God has already established His way of salvation and his method of deliverance from evil. And it can happen in no other way than through an individual's faith in Jesus Christ.

God is not going to change His mind and do something different. Neither is God going to say to His Son, "I'm sorry, Jesus, for sending you to the cross to provide deliverance for everyone who would have faith in you. I have decided to provide deliverance in a different way. Instead of delivering only those who place their faith in what was done on the cross, I have decided to just rip evil out of the earth. Son, I have decided to bypass what you did in your earthly ministry and by my grace, I will just remove evil out of the way. People will no longer have to place their individual faith in you. I'll take the condition of this sinful world into my own hands."

The main concept behind this prophecy disagrees with what the Word says about the last days. The Bible clearly shows us that the world is going to get darker in the last days – not lighter (Isaiah 60:2).

This man experienced a vision which should have been tested immediately according to 1 John 4:1-3, but it wasn't.

"Beloved, do not believe every spirit, but test the spirits, whether they are of God; because many false prophets have gone out into the world. By this you know the Spirit of God: Every spirit that confesses that Jesus Christ has come in the flesh is of God, and every spirit that does not confess that Jesus Christ has come in the flesh is not of God. And this is the spirit of the Antichrist, which you have heard was coming, and is now already in the world" (1 John 4:1-3).

FLAKEY PROPHECIES

He exalted his own experience above the written revelation of Christ and yielded to carnal ideas. Much of the Charismatic Church was deceived because this prophecy was featured on a major Christian television network, *TBN,* for several months. Not one major Charismatic leader came forward with enough

Chapter Eight

discernment and boldness to publicly test or expose it before it became public. As a result, many immature Christians were led astray. Leaders like this will eventually have to be exposed for leading people away from the true revelation of Christ.

I know by experience, and by biblical understanding, that I too yielded to wrong manifestations and flakey prophecies. That is why I can say with conviction that this pastor's whole experience was the result of yielding to a false vision.

The true Holy Spirit would never bypass truth and bring a vision based on an entirely new anti-Jesus concept. Furthermore, the grace of God would never disregard the need for faith in Christ.

We may assume that this kind of prophecy is uncommon, but that is not the case. Many Charismatic prophecies conveniently bypass God's original plan of salvation. Evidence of this is found in prophetic words like, "God is going to peel back the darkness from men's eyes and they will be swept into the kingdom by the thousands."

We seem to forget that Jesus is the light. If we reject Him, we remain in darkness and there isn't anything God will do about it. If God broke into people's lives and peeled back the darkness, then He would be saying, "The light of the revelation of Christ is not enough." To open men's eyes, God would have to add to the completed plan of salvation.

To confess, "Jesus did not reveal the full majesty and brilliance of the light of God's Word," and "God is doing a new thing," exposes a misunderstanding of the reason why Jesus came in the flesh.

DRUNK IN THE SPIRIT

We have all heard of people falling down or stumbling around drunk in the spirit. The Toronto Blessing and the

Brownsville Assembly of God revival in Pensacola, Florida, has brought international attention to this phenomena.

We, as a church and the movement we were a part of, were experiencing many similar manifestations several years before it became popular.

Where did we acquire this doctrine? Well, we concocted it from one obscure interpretation of a single reference of Scripture in the second chapter of the book of Acts. We combined it with carnal references to the "wine" of the Holy Spirit. And when we heard it preached and verified by men of renown we all jumped on the bandwagon. Well, maybe you didn't, but I did.

Majoring on Minors

This shouldn't surprise us. There are many doctrines that the Church believes which are founded upon single Scriptures. We often make major teachings out of minor references.

We also do the opposite. Sometimes we give only minor attention to the major teachings of the Bible. For instance, even though Jesus Christ is the major revelation of the whole Bible, few of us see any need to enter the depth of studying the many prophetic references that point to Christ in the Old Testament. We fail to see that studying the references to Jesus is the key to understanding all Scripture. Therefore, the most important emphasis of the entire Bible is treated as simple and basic.

How is this problem going to be uncovered? When we find out that we are ignoring the full revelation of Christ and admit that we have ascribed many un-Christ-like attributes to God. We use single references and half-truths to portray God's character, while the whole revelation of God's true character is found fully revealed in Christ. But we don't seem to understand that. We seem to treat Christ's earthly ministry as only a partial revelation of the glory of God. Nothing could be further from the truth.

Chapter Eight

NEW WINE OF THE HOLY SPIRIT

The "drunk in the Spirit" doctrine, reveals a common, traditional habit of "majoring on minors and minoring on majors."

This reference in Acts (which has been misinterpreted and used to substantiate the experience of spiritual drunkenness) is found in the setting of chapter two. It refers the early Church believers who were filled with the Holy Spirit and began to speak in other tongues as the Spirit gave them utterance. Further on in the text, skeptics entered the scene.

"Others mocking said, 'They are full of new wine" (Acts 2:13).

SOBER PEOPLE DON'T STAND OUT

The mockers did not understand what was going on so they assumed that the believers were drunk. What else would worldly people think? That is always their excuse for people who do strange things. As far as the worldly mind goes, sober people don't stand out in a crowd. Only the inebriated are bold and uninhibited. Therefore, to them, these bold believers, who were preaching the Gospel in many languages, were obviously enhanced and motivated by the empowering effects of liquor. What else could these mockers have said but, "They are full of new wine?"

Today, a few preachers have taken this Scripture out of context and have claimed "Holy Ghost drunkenness" as a scriptural idea. We have blindly and willingly followed their leading by acting drunk in Christian meetings.

We have not rightly divided the Word. From that false assumption of the meaning of Acts chapter two, we have built a whole new movement and have concluded that this Scripture was referring to believers staggering around like drunken men.

One puff of wind from a teaching based on an obscure reference and off we go. The rest of the context and the rest of the Bible mean nothing to us!

Yet, in defense against the mocking remark, Peter said, "these are not drunk as you suppose."

The drunken display seen in churches today ventures way beyond what Jesus taught. Again, we have transgressed the doctrine of Christ.

"Whoever transgresses and does not abide in the doctrine of Christ does not have God. He who abides in the doctrine of Christ has both the Father and the Son" (2 John 1:9).

Drunk on False Prophecies

If we want to talk about the difference between majors and minors, I have found *more* Scriptures with reference to being intoxicated with false visions and false prophesies than I have found about being "drunk in the Holy Spirit."

"They are drunk, but not with wine; They stagger, but not with intoxicating drink. For the Lord has poured out on you The spirit of deep sleep, And has closed your eyes, namely, the prophets..." (Isaiah 29:9-10).

"But they also have erred through wine, And through intoxicating drink are out of the way; The priest and the prophet have erred through intoxicating drink, They are swallowed up by wine, They are out of the way through intoxicating drink; They err in vision, they stumble in judgment" (Isaiah 28:7).

Interestingly, the reference in Isaiah chapter twenty-eight verse seven seems to contrast with verse eleven.

"For with stammering lips and another tongue He will speak to this people, To whom He said, 'This is the rest with which You may cause the weary to rest,' And, 'This is the refreshing'; Yet they would not hear..." (Isaiah 28:11,12).

Chapter Eight

Why wouldn't they listen to the Lord? Why were they willfully rejecting God's method of teaching? It was because they were so busy getting drunk on false prophecies that they missed out on God's true, prophetic refreshing – the simple Word of God taught line upon line, and precept upon precept to hungry believers (Isaiah 28:9-13).

The intoxication of the false prophets puts forth a different spiritual manifestation than that of those who would be filled with the true Spirit of God. Drunkenness seems to belong to the false prophets, but not to the true people of God. By looking at the manifestations of the whole worldwide "River" movement, it is obvious that we may be repeating history and are following the blunders and mistakes of our forefathers and the erring prophets of the Children of Israel. We are basking in our own soulish intoxication while the real refreshing of the Holy Spirit is being rejected as boring, mundane, and uninteresting.

LAUGHING IN THE SPIRIT

At first, we as a church did our best to yield to the new laughing revival and tried to get into the drunk in the Spirit phenomena. We participated in large gatherings where the "new anointing" was being distributed and we taught this new wind of doctrine in our own church. But, as time went on, we discovered that the Bible did not substantiate this doctrine.

Not only did we find that these concepts lacked scriptural backing, but we also found that they disagreed with Jesus. He was the ultimate example of a man filled with the spirit of gladness, yet we didn't find these laughing manifestations in His life and ministry.

"You have loved righteousness and hated lawlessness; Therefore God, Your God, has anointed You With the oil of gladness more than Your companions" (Hebrew 1:9).

We found that the doctrine of laughing in the Spirit contradicted the anointed life of Christ. It is obvious that Jesus was anointed with the oil of gladness more than any man who will ever live and yet there isn't any proof in the Bible of Jesus laughing hysterically or imparting it onto anyone else. If we truly want to be filled with the joy of the Lord, why don't we pattern ourselves after Jesus who hated evil and loved righteousness.

Now, I am not saying that we shouldn't laugh, cry, or be emotional. These characteristics are a strong part of our humanity. Jesus cried, shouted, and became angry. But to say that "laughing" is a supernatural manifestation of the Holy Spirit is truly a leap.

INNER HEALING

I'm sure that many people do not realize that the Toronto Blessing, and other revival centers featuring "the river" or "the refreshing," happen to feature similar kinds of manifestations because their thoughts and teachings on deliverance are all established in the roots of inner healing.

Inner healing is a teaching which suggests that there is a need for believers to heal their past after they are born again or go through great emotional experiences in order to be delivered from the haunting ghosts of their previous life.

We, as a church, were also taken in with this kind of teaching for a while. Therefore, when counseling or taking people through deliverance, we often blamed many peoples' problems on their past. The result was, a lack of personal responsibility of repenting or turning to God: it was always someone else's fault. When we ministered to them, we didn't tell them who they were in Christ but rather focused on the old man and the hurts of the past. It wasn't until later that I discovered that this attitude rejected the whole purpose of the cross.

Chapter Eight

In facing some of their problems or memories of the past, people become desperate. Instead of realizing or learning that by faith their past is past and their sins, problems, mistakes, and offenses were nailed to the cross, they tend to seek experiences that outwardly verify the healing of their past. This opens them up to demonic activity because they refuse to accept new creation realities by faith.

Their refusal to accept the finished work of Christ on the cross isn't totally their fault alone. Leaders of the Church like to keep an interdependence between the hurting, who think they need counseling, and the counselors, who need to be needed. These leaders would be the last to admit, "There's no need to heal the old works of the flesh." If they admitted to the seeking Christian, "There's no longer any need to deal with the past other than placing your faith in the finished work of the cross," then their counseling services and inner healing ministries would disappear.

THE TRUTH WILL SET YOU FREE

One of the Scriptures, which has constantly been misapplied and used to substantiate inner healing, is;

"And you shall know the truth, and the truth shall make you free" (John 8:32).

This classic Scripture has been taken out of context so many times in sermons and teachings that we hardly notice the deception. The reason this Scripture can be quoted out of context without detection, is because we don't read our Bibles like we should. We tend to use interpretations of Bible verses we have heard from others rather than the Bible verses we have read and studied for ourselves. We seem to approve of opinions and teachings we have often heard in our own circles without questioning them or without reading what the Bible has to say about them.

If Scriptures are misapplied continuously, then we learn a bad habit: we learn to approve of wrong interpretations. If we don't study and search the Bible for confirmation then they obviously will deceive us.

Based on popular phrases like, "the truth will set you free," people have been led to believe that it refers to personal prophetic words. If they experience a vision or if they receive a word concerning something out of their past – that they had either forgotten or never knew – then that special word must be the "truth" about their past that needed to be revealed. They believe this is the meaning behind the verse, "and you will know the truth and the truth will set you free." It is assumed that the vision or the word was truly "revelation" about something long forgotten. But that is not the true meaning of the word "truth."

THE TRUTH IS HIS WORD

When Jesus spoke these words, "And you shall know the truth, and the truth shall make you free," He was speaking about knowing and understanding His Word. If you continue in His Word, you will come to know the truth and the truth you understand will set you free. Anyone who will continue to learn about what Jesus did on the cross will realize that their past is gone. It was nailed to the tree with Jesus. The whole concept behind inner healing opposes the objectives of Christ. The reality and purpose of the cross is belittled and pseudo-deliverance is promoted in its place.

FABRICATED PROBLEMS

In one case, a young Christian man traveled to special meetings at the Toronto Blessing. When he returned, he claimed that he was set free from three demons. The adults who knew the

Chapter Eight

young man asked, "when did he get these three demons – was it while he was traveling on the plane to Toronto?"

This is a good question. For surely the folks who knew the young man would have been aware of his problems. And if he had three demons, other Christians should have been aware of his needs.

The sad thing about this story is it is all too common. People seem to be easily convinced of their need for deliverance when a problem is fabricated in the midst of a highly emotional revival meeting. The result is; many people experience bogus deliverances at these meetings because their problems are bogus and manufactured on the spot. These folks have little proof of their exposed problems because it is based on visions, words, prophecies, or someone else's opinion. Many of the so-called miracles begin as fabricated needs accompanied by fabricated manifestations. Only the immature and the undiscerning are impressed with the so-called results. In all of this, the work of the cross Christ is being bypassed.

INNER HEALING SESSIONS

Many who are involved in inner healing claim, "The strange things that happen during healing sessions are the work of the Holy Spirit." But the true Holy Spirit isn't going to disagree with the finished work of the cross. Why would He reveal something out of our past if it was buried with Christ Jesus and we were raised up by the Holy Spirit to live for God? It doesn't agree with God's original plan of salvation. God sent Jesus to the earth in the flesh to die for our flesh and get it out of the way. He didn't send Jesus to die for just a portion of our sins and offenses and then leave the rest up to the "Inner Healing" specialists. Inner Healing seems to suggest that God's salvation plan fell short of total deliverance.

A hurting Christian doesn't need soulish sensations, false counseling, or visions of their unknown past in order to be free. They need to know the truth about what Jesus did for them on the cross and then choose to die with Him.

FLESH VS. SPIRIT

The reason most people seek an alternative form of healing their past is because they won't let the old man go to the grave. The old man is the flesh. The new man is the recreated spirit.

Most of us assume that the biblical term *flesh* refers only to our physical bodies but that isn't the most accurate application or interpretation. *Flesh* refers to an attitude within the human race which constantly opposes God while it exalts the ability of man. The flesh, of course, does not want to die or be put aside. The flesh screams in terror at the very thought of being crucified on the cross with Jesus.

The Christian who realizes that the war isn't between the past and their present feelings will truly start to overcome. Christians must see the real battleground in their own lives is the self-exalting attitude of the flesh versus the Jesus exalting revelation of the Spirit.

In fact, trying to make Christians feel better about themselves is not a proper solution. It is a dangerous shortcut if Christians assume that their freedom is accomplished by replacing bad feelings with good feelings. It is little more than pretending to deal with the flesh while exalting our fleshly feelings. And ultimately, it is a counterfeit victory.

By analyzing the teachings in the Church concerning the cross, we find a misunderstanding of the true purpose of crucifixion. Most Christians believe that Jesus died on the cross for them as a substitute, so they wouldn't have to die for their sins. That supposition is only partly right. We will not fully comprehend the power of the cross until we learn how to die to the flesh with Christ on the cross (Gal. 2:20). There will be no resurrection in our lives until we understand the death of man's carnal ways.

"Therefore, since Christ suffered for us in the flesh, arm yourselves also with the same mind, for he who has suffered in the flesh has ceased from sin, that he no longer should live the rest of his time in the flesh for the lusts of men, but for the will of God" (1 Peter 4:1,2).

"Likewise you also, reckon yourselves to be dead indeed to sin, but alive to God in Christ Jesus our Lord" (Romans 6:11).

The fleshly soul wars against the truth and the desires of the flesh lust against the Spirit (Gal. 5:17). We must renew our minds with the truth: "We are dead in Christ." Sometimes feelings can be misleading; especially when our souls don't feel saved. Our feelings don't have anything to do with salvation, but our souls are so accustomed to leading us through *emotionalism;* we struggle to bow to the truth. Therefore, in order to avoid the struggle, we seek an alternative way of feeling healed and saved.

In all of this, the Devil is very active. He knows we are refusing to seek after truth because he can see we are not reading our Bibles for the answers. He can see that we're seeking to *feel* salvation in our soul instead of *believing* the truth in our hearts.

The soul realm is the Devil's favorite arena. It is his specialty. He loves to seduce the carnal soul through carnal teachings and experiences conveniently provided for us by carnal leaders. We are vulnerable because we aren't lovers of truth – we are lovers of pleasure. We would rather feel better than deal with reality.

The reason these self-made ministers are able to tempt us away from the truth is; we refuse to die on the cross to our sensual and soulish ways.

"For the time will come when they will not endure sound doctrine, but according to their own desires, because they have itching ears, they will heap up for themselves teachers; and they will turn their ears away from the truth, and be turned aside to fables" (2 Timothy 4:3-4).

WE EXALT OUR OWN EXPERIENCES

The reason the Church is being taken in by spiritual goosebumps, false signs, and soulish wonders is because we believe what we see with our eyes or experience in our soul much stronger than what we read in the Word. In fact, we have come to the place where we like being moved in our soul much more than we like being challenged by the truth. It is evident in our classification of what we call *spiritual*. If one our favorite ministers tells us a moving story or a Gospel music group pulls on our emotions, we experience something which is defined as *satisfaction*. Our souls have been stirred. But we are still lacking the truth and we seem to be happy with that.

Why do we elevate our experiences far above the reality of the truth? Why do so many Christians fall into this trap? In recent years, I have heard from ministers and read many articles from preachers who have unknowingly verified and approved of false signs and wonders simply because they experienced similar sensations in their own ministry.

I have done the same thing myself. I've defended strange manifestations in my own ministry simply because I yielded to them on a regular basis. Since I exalted experience above knowledge, I ignorantly defended deception. In other words, I approved of extra-biblical experiences which had nothing in common with the miracles of Jesus simply because I respected my experiences more than Christ.

This is defined in Christian circles as being *pragmatic*. Pragmatism occurs when we exalt our thoughts, our feelings, and our experiences to a divine level. "If I think it or feel it, it must be from God."

Chapter Eight

Some of my peers have claimed, "I had questioned the whole idea of laughing in the spirit until I was preaching in a meeting, and all of a sudden, people began to laugh in the middle of my sermon. It was a sign from Heaven. This proves that it is from God because it happened in my meeting."

Experiences Do Not Equal Truth

Since when do we make our own experiences the foundation for truth? Since when are we supposed to accept manifestations without testing them properly? And since when do we think that only good things happen in our meetings?

Do preachers think themselves to be unaffected by other spirits? Do they assume that everything supernatural they encounter, experience, and prophesy in their meetings is from God? Just because it happens in their meetings does not mean God is giving it a stamp of approval. All manifestations must be tested according to the Word.

Another minister might say, "Yes, I remember many years ago we had a similar experience. We were having special meetings and had a great revival. In one of the meetings, people began to uncontrollably laugh and cry. It was really something. What we hear of happening today, in the Toronto Blessing and the Brownsville Revival, are the same kind of manifestations we encountered years ago. It must be of God."

They are using their own experiences and the experiences of their spiritual predecessors as the new standard of measurement instead of Jesus.

Carnal Prejudice

Our own Charismatic ignorance became evident when we used our own brand of "laughing in the spirit" to judge and separate ourselves from the "Toronto Blessing" and other groups which had similar manifestations. I've heard many preachers say the same thing, "Our laughing is of God and theirs is not." This is not spiritual discernment. This is carnal prejudice! Nevertheless, it is very common among the many *camps* of the Charismatic Church. We all think our own manifestations are better than everyone else's. The sad truth is, very few of these so-called new miracles are Christ-like. Therefore, many of them do not demonstrate the true Gospel or agree with Christ's brand of miracles.

By letting these laughing experiences go untested, we will now use them as new premise or foundation for truth. All of these experiences including the previous ones, which happened in the late 1800's and the early 1900's have become a part of the Pentecostal/Charismatic church's documented history. These documented manifestations should be examined and tested according to Scriptures like 1 John 4:1-3. According to that test, none of the miracles, which people experienced in Jesus' ministry, ever included laughing, shaking, barking, or crying in the spirit. None of them ever included falling down in emotional hysteria or dancing in the spirit. When Jesus ministered to people, they were physically healed. Healing was never manifested as a soulish pre-miracle feeling or experience. But, for some reason, we seem to have more respect for our denominational forefathers and their carnal antics.

How Can the Devil Deceive Leaders?

The Devil is progressive with deception. He knows he can't come in overnight and manifest himself in the temple. He must take his time. If he is able to penetrate meetings today and exalt wrong manifestations, then he knows he can take it a little further later on. The unholy manifestations in the Charismatic Church are stronger lying wonders today, only because we

Chapter Eight

received an introductory lie, years ago.

We tend to continue to build upon these false foundations because we are experience-based. It is a perpetual problem. What I have seen happen in the *Refreshing*, the *Toronto Blessing*, and the *Brownsville Revival* are just stronger lying wonders based on things accepted in the "Azusa Street Revival," and in the Wesley, Finney, and Edward's meetings." Weak anti-Jesus manifestations in the 1900's only prepared us for stronger seductions in the Church today.

What should have happened with the miracles of "Azusa Street" and other revivals is obvious. They should have been compared to Jesus' miracles. Then the false miracles would have been exposed and we would have been prepared to discern stronger deceptions today. We should have settled long ago which miracles confessed "Jesus came in the flesh" and which ones did not.

While we think that all these past revivals were moves of God, we must be corrected to realize that God has only been involved in one movement since the beginning of the Church Age. He has been building His Church and calling His people to return to Him through the revelation of Jesus. There was truth in the early Church and there is truth today. There was deception in the early Church and there is deception today. Even the Old Testament shows the ongoing struggle between the false and the true. Things haven't changed much.

"But there were also false prophets among the people, even as there will be false teachers among you, who will secretly bring in destructive heresies, even denying the Lord who bought them, and bring on themselves swift destruction" (2 Peter 2:1).

This is still the Church Age! The Holy Spirit is still doing the same thing He was sent to do – glorify the Lord Jesus Christ and lead us into truth. Only the truth will set us free from our own deceptions!

◆ Chapter Nine

FAMILIAR SPIRITS EXPOSED

For many years, I heard very little teaching on *familiar spirits*. Only glimpses of the subject were given to us as "nuggets" in the middle of someone's sermon or teaching. A little knowledge is almost as dangerous as none at all. We were never taught the truth, therefore, we were easily led into many false assumptions concerning familiar spirits.

Word of Faith preachers taught us that familiar spirits were *familiar* with us. Others taught us that they were *secretary spirits* keeping track of our mistakes and blunders in order to trap us in our patterns of sin. Spiritual Warfare teachers told us that familiar spirits were *ancestral spirits* who attached curses to family lineage.

Is it really true that familiar spirits are evil spirits who are familiar with us? Are they demons who are watching us in order to accumulate information? Are they ancestral spirits keeping data about our families in order to use it against us? Are familiar spirits active through family curses?

We need some accurate biblical teaching on familiar spirits in order to answer these questions.

As I started to look at this, I found much more in the Word on this subject than I first suspected. It was not just an obscure topic – it was immense. The subject of familiar spirits brought freedom to me because as I studied this, I discovered that I had been yielding to spiritual lies and I wasn't even aware of it.

In the Old Testament, the familiar spirits were the medium spirits behind false prophets among God's people. And I believe they are still active both within and without the Christian Church of today. They were the supernatural miracle workers sent to deceive. Familiar spirits were the power behind the signs and wonders of the false prophets. They were the source for the spiritual inspiration behind false visions and false prophecies. They were the fountainhead for spiritual experiences which bypassed God's Word. Today a similar thing is happening which is yielding miracles which are essentially anti-Jesus and pseudo-Jesus manifestations.

In the Old Testament, the spirits behind the false prophets were called familiar spirits. In the New Testament, the spirits behind the false prophets are simply called seducing spirits, the spirits of error, or the spirits of Antichrist" (1 Timothy 4:1, 1 John 4:1-6)

IMPOSTORS

The Bible is full of information about these medium spirits. This allows us to study their wiles in the Bible and find out how they work. They may appear under different names; but their works, manifestations, and their deceptive ways are found both in the Old and New Testaments. We must, therefore, be alert and be prepared because Scripture warns us that these deceiving spirits and false manifestations will be found among God's people in the last days.

Jesus taught us about the activities of these impostors and showed us how they would mimic the true anointing.

"For false christs and false prophets will rise and show great signs and wonders to deceive, if possible, even the elect" (Matthew 24:24).

How is it possible to lead the very elect away from the truth? An even more important question might be, "How in the world will those who know Christ be misled to follow a false Christ?" If the elect includes leaders, are they going to be deceived as well?

First of all, we need to be honest. Not everything supernatural that happens in the Church is from God. We need to admit to ourselves that we have experienced and have believed in things which are un-Christ-like. There is deception in the body of Christ today: we need to stop pointing our finger at everyone else. In particular, we need to stop blaming the leaders of other camps. False teachings are not found only in isolated cases outside of our own church affiliations. Deception and false teachings have been sown as tares throughout the entire field of the Church. The flakes are evenly distributed.

Many prominent leaders, throughout the entire spectrum of the Church, have received unscriptural visions, false prophecies, and extra-biblical experiences. These false experiences are manifestations of the "flesh" working in covenant relationship with familiar spirits. And it is happening within the setting of the Church.

Take Heed

If Jesus' words of warning, found in Matthew chapter twenty-four, indicate to us how deceptive these spirits would be, we had better listen to Him and take heed.

"For false christs and false prophets will rise and show great signs and wonders to deceive, if possible, even the elect" (Matthew 24:24).

"Now the Spirit expressly says that in the latter times some will depart from the faith, giving heed to deceiving spirits and doctrines of demons" (1 Timothy 4:1).

Familiar spirits and their New Testament counterparts are key enemy spirits which must be identified in our battle against deception.

We can't go on assuming that the only purpose behind familiar spirits is to be familiar with us. We can't go on assuming that familiar spirits are ancestral spirits attaching themselves to family lineage.

The true meaning of "familiar" is linked more to the Hebrew definition than to the English. The words *familiar spirits* are translated from the Hebrew word "obe" which is a perverted form of "ab." "Ab" was the Hebrew word for "father" and it was a term of respect and honor. Many famous Bible characters' names began with this prefix; Abimelech, Abinadab, Absalom, etc. Abraham's name began with the same prefix "ab." His name was a respected name which meant "father of many" or "father of the faithful."

Baby Talk

Inherent within the word "obe" was the idea of prattling the father's name. To "prattle" means to talk like a baby or to speak many empty things. It also means, "babel" and "confusion." It is normal for a baby to speak "baby talk." It's normal for a little one to not know how to speak their father's name clearly or respectfully.

However, it isn't normal for an adult to act this way. It can seem very disrespectful and even mocking, for an adult to act like a baby and prattle their father's name.

Immature leaders who claim to be anointed by the Spirit of God – but speak many empty words – are the "obe" of today.

They claim to be sent by the Father, but their empty words expose their true character. They mimic and speak many religious words, but the respect for the Word is notably absent.

"God, who at various times and in various ways spoke in time past to the fathers by the prophets, has in these last days spoken to us by His Son..." (Hebrews 1:1-2).

Jesus is the Word of God made flesh and He is the Word sent from the Father. God, in these last days, has clearly spoken to us by His Son. This is the Father's words: we need to respect and understand them.

False prophets under the influence of familiar spirits or antichrist spirits do not fully preach the Gospel. They preach many other things. They speak many empty spiritual words, spiritual baby talk, nonsense, and endless prattle. Spiritual babies cannot discern what the empty words are really saying. Only believers who will fill themselves with the Father's Word will discern these false leaders.

Supernatural Nonsense

Familiar spirits (obe) also means to sound empty like a hollow water-skin or wineskin. The picture this word is painting is not the actual physical sound of words coming from an empty wineskin. The idea portrayed here is: the words themselves are "empty." They are empty barrels. They don't contain the true Gospel. They are hollow meaningless words which result in supernatural nonsense.

There is a bunch of nonsense being promoted as substance in the Church today, but because of our hunger, we are gullible enough to take in anything which closely resembles, sounds like, or looks spiritual. Sadly, we are ending up with counterfeit sensations, speaking idle words, and experiencing a lot of empty-headed spiritual fantasies. There is a great contrast between what

Chapter Nine

we are advocating as from God when compared to the true character of the Father as revealed through the Son. The Church is being sold a bunch of fluff as substance. We are being taken in by "baby talk" and "prattle." It's time to grow up.

The sad thing about this is most of these experiences can hold a tight grip on us because they are associated with or accompanied by very strong sensations. To dismiss many of these manifestations as just an overactive imagination is to deny the existence of spiritual forces. Familiar spirits and antichrist spirits are not something we should belittle. Denial in this game is spiritually deadly.

◆ Chapter Ten

DIVINATION

Familiar spirits are also classed as the spirits of divination. Divination is known as looking into the spirit realm to know the past, the present, or the future. It's the supernatural manifestations of bogus prophecies, lying wonders, and false visions which gives a false impression of spiritual insight. It makes us believe that anointed ministers can know the hidden unknown secrets of our hearts or even expose forces and influences in our lives of which we were never aware.

It's interesting to see what God says about divination and the prophets who were involved in it. In Ezekiel chapter thirteen, we see the concept of divination being directly linked to prophets and leaders who were among God's people but no longer speaking the Word of God.

"Thus says the Lord God: "Woe to the foolish prophets, who follow their own spirit and have seen nothing" (Ezekiel 13:3).

"They have envisioned futility and false divination..." (Ezekiel 13:6).

This reflects the Hebrew word for familiar spirits because "obe" means "empty or hollow." It can also mean "to mumble."

Chapter Ten

Now, it is apparent that false prophets of today do not mumble. But it is also apparent that false prophets can articulate words that muffle and hide God's true purposes – a lot of spiritual-sounding words that say nothing. In other words: the empty spiritual words come across like a fine prophecy. It represents the false prophet who flatters the people of God instead of telling them the truth. They declare "peace, peace" when there is no peace.

A word of blessing is a dangerous prophecy when the people are far from God. The people of God may need to hear, "you must return to the Lord."

I recently attended a minister's conference, which featured a "prophet" who gave personal prophecies. During the meetings, I had the opportunity to dialogue with a pastor who was opening up to some of the new revival concepts and strange manifestations. He was actively pursuing these new things for his church. I was able to share my side of the story and it seemed like I was getting through to him. But during one of the meetings, the prophet called the pastor out of the congregation and flattered him with a wonderful prophecy which said, "God is with you, You are seeking the right things for your church. And if you continue, your meetings will increase to five hours or more. Your influence will increase in your city, it will spread to your province and then to your nation."

So I ask you, "Who is this pastor going to listen to now – my counsel to stay away from these strange doctrines – or the prophet's encouraging words of flattery?" Instead of exposing the popular false teachings of today for the benefit of the pastor, the prophet stroked his pride and built him up with foolishness.

PROPHETIC FLATTERY

A true prophet wouldn't flatter such a man. He would confront him and tell him the truth. Yet I know the false prophet was convinced that this was the word he should give. I know how strong the motivation can be to conjure up prophetic words for the congregation. He didn't know it, but he was tickling the man's ears while under the influence of seducing spirits.

SPEAKING THROUGH A HOLE IN THE GROUND

Another characteristic of familiar spirits is further revealed in the book of Isaiah.

"You shall be brought down, you shall speak out of the ground; your speech shall be low, out of the dust; Your voice shall be like a medium's (familiar spirit), out of the ground; and your speech shall whisper out of the dust" (Isaiah 29:4).

Can you imagine trying to hear someone who is speaking out of a hole in the ground? I don't think there's anything that can smother a person's voice like layers of earth between you and them. Even if a person shouts the message it may remain unintelligible; so hard to understand that you may have to strain to hear what they are saying.

This is further insight into the character of familiar spirits. Their spiritual message cannot be easily understood.

Of course, you realize we're not talking about the actual physical sound of the voice. If a preacher stood in a pulpit and began making unintelligible sounds with his voice, then we wouldn't need any discernment to conclude that you are not going to stay around for the rest of the meeting.

What we are talking about is the lack of clarity in the spiritual message. Is the Gospel of Jesus Christ coming through loud and clear or do we have to strain to know what the preacher is talking about? Familiar spirits manifest through messages which appear prophetic but do not clearly reveal the Word of God. The spiritual words are audible, but the message of the Gospel is vague. The preacher may even shout his message, but the spiritual content of his words are still empty of truth. They might as well speak through a hole in the ground. The revelation of God's Word is mysteriously missing. It is like an empty bottle; there's nothing there to satisfy the spirit man. Only the flesh would be entertained by such emptiness.

CHARMERS

"They will consult the idols and the charmers, the mediums and the sorcerers" (Isaiah 19:3).

The definition for charmers mean; "to whisper, low speech, and noiseless speaking." Charmers also operated their wiles through the channel of familiar spirits. Their soft ways are likened to the subtlety of a spider's web.

"Charmers" are those who "moved and spoke softly and gently." Incantations given by the charmers were gentle, sweet, and soft.

This is a very accurate description of the kind of antichrist spirits that I've seen in action. False teachers who are under the influence of antichrist spirits are real charmers. They can be very controlling by their soft approach and their gentle persuasion. They can seem so sweet, loving, and kind while they spin their web of deception. You hardly notice that the trap is closing in.

Who in their right mind would dare challenge the doctrines of such a sweet and gentle charmer? Who would dare expose them as false or accuse them of being motivated by demons? When you challenge their doctrine, don't be surprised if people turn on you and accuse you of not walking in the same level of love as these seducers. As you listen to their spiritual message, you will find the simple clarity of the Gospel mysteriously missing, almost silent in a way. The truth of the Gospel and the revelation of Jesus Christ – a mere whisper. What they are saying is only a shadow of the truth. But don't be surprised when many around you are taken in with their soft words.

The Devil is a snake. He is cunning and moves very cautiously before he strikes. But he can strike with deadly accuracy once he is close enough to his victim. It is almost like watching someone trapped by a spell. It overtakes them ever so slowly and quietly.

"Who has bewitched you that you should not obey the truth...?" (Galatians 3:1).

I have seen people mesmerized and fascinated with personal prophecies and false signs and wonders. Their comments would reflect this after a flakey church meeting, "Such a wonderful service." They were spellbound and charmed with the alleged supernatural words and manifestations. This may sound redundant but when are we going realize – just because it appears to be supernatural doesn't mean it's from God?

Witchcraft in the Church

One of the manifestations of familiar spirits in the Old Testament was "witchcraft." The definition for witchcraft is, "to gather clouds or to soothsay or to act covertly or undercover."

Sometimes a message can sound very spiritual but the true meaning behind that message can be very cloudy. In other words, the gray just won't go away.

The purpose of witchcraft is to mislead under cloud cover. Immature Christians who are misled by false manifestations are misled only because of the confusion of the cloud cover.

You may say to yourself, "I haven't got the foggiest idea of what this preacher is saying." But you keep listening because you think the preacher is more open to the Spirit than you are.

As the knowledge of God's Word concerning familiar spirits began to make sense to me, I was able to discern what was

Chapter Ten

going on. What surprised me was the fact that deception was more common among Charismatic leaders than I had imagined.

Let's make it clear. Jesus Christ is our message. God's parables contain the power to change lives. Meanwhile, our own parables only entertain. Empty words do not belong inside the Church. The Church has yielded to these things in the name of the "prophetic anointing" long enough. The true prophetic anointing isn't cloudy. The message is clear and alive. Revelation 19:10 says, "for the testimony of Jesus is the spirit of prophecy." Let's get it straight, He is our message!

◆ Chapter Eleven

SPIRITS OF THE DEAD

One of the other interesting definitions for familiar spirits is "conjuring up spirits of the dead." Now, I know we would never knowingly or purposely do such a thing; but, nevertheless, many Christians do this out of religious habit.

A good example of this is the popular Catholic concept of praying to the saints. The idea comes from the concept of Christian leaders and other saintly men and women who have passed on and are supposedly in Heaven. We call them "saints" and pray to them, who in turn are supposed to plead with a "judgmental Christ" to loosen His blessings upon us.

Within liturgical Charismatic circles, visions of Mary, idols that bleed, and supernatural saintly visits in the night are on the rise. But be warned, this isn't the work of the Holy Spirit. The purpose of these visions and visitations is to keep us in religious captivity, separated from the true concept of Christ. Again, this is the powerful influence of wrong teachings.

Often, these people will experience something moving which convinces them that the supernatural experience was infallible proof that what they are seeing was from God. The dearly departed don't actually come back from the dead; but, in reality, the Word of God is pushed aside to make room for a new voice.

We must remember something very important. The Devil isn't anti-religion, anti-signs and wonders, or anti-spiritual experiences. He is anti-Jesus. If the Devil can keep us occupied with empty spiritual experiences, he can keep us from Christ. This is his ultimate goal.

The Devil isn't threatened when we pray in the name of Mary or when we pray to a Saint. In fact, he likes it. He is only defeated when we identify with the name of Jesus and understand what that name represents.

So what if we find a set of keys when we've prayed to "Saint Whoever" for help? Is it supernatural proof that what we are doing is from God? The Devil doesn't care if we find the set of keys or not. If he could, he would even send his demons to help us. All he cares about is keeping us from the revelation of Jesus by beguiling us with false miracles.

KING SAUL YIELDED TO FAMILIAR SPIRITS

King Saul is a good example of what happens to people when they open up to new voices. He was guilty of yielding to familiar spirits and conjuring up spirits of the dead.

He had rebelled against God's prophetic Word and wouldn't repent. As a result, God was no longer speaking to him. This left a great void in his life.

During the time when he served God, he knew his future was secure. But when King Saul was no longer serving God – he didn't know what the future held in store for him.

He knew things would go well as long as he was submitted to God. But when he was cut off from God, because of his rebellion, he didn't know if things were going to work in his favor.

This void desperately needed attention and since God wasn't talking to him, he decided to consult a woman who had a familiar spirit (1 Samuel 27:5-19).

The women "conjured up" a voice from Saul's past, the voice of the prophet Samuel, a voice from the grave. This was a huge step backward for the King and as far as God was concerned, this was the last straw. Because of this, God took away his kingdom and began looking for someone else to lead the Children of Israel.

How did Saul the King come to the place where he would stoop so low? Why did he turn to divination instead of turning back to the Lord?

Rebellion was the reason for Saul's fall. He had been told by the prophet Samuel, "Rebellion is as the sin of witchcraft." But Saul didn't repent. The spiritual void in Saul's life cried out for attention and since he wouldn't turn from his rebellion, he opened up to familiar spirits.

Revival Seeking Christians

A similar thing happens to today's revival seeking Christians. When we are first born again, we were made aware of a new realm. We realize there is a spirit realm. As we grow spiritually, we are thrilled to hear the voice of God as His Word comes alive to us. But when we rebel and grow hard to the voice of His Word, it leaves a spiritual void in our lives. Since we won't go back to God's Word, we seek another way of fulfilling that void. We open up to the spirit realm instead of the inspired Word of God!

The false experiences that follow, often distract people from the Word and reinforce their rebellion. I've seen rebellious sheep leave the fold because of this. The interesting thing was, these people were attracted to the very thing we warned them about.

Chapter Eleven

The good teaching they had received about the revelation of Christ, how to discern antichrist spirits, deception, and emptiness, seemed to mean nothing to them. They were able to go to another church and experience incredible spiritual things and backslide all at the same time. These people could remain in their rebellion and fall down under the power, get spiritually drunk, and laugh in the spirit all night.

It is my observation that rebellious Christians seem to be more receptive to these false signs and wonders than others. I have seen people refuse to leave their sin and still long for the voice of the Spirit. They seek out churches where their sins aren't known – usually it's a church which allows many kinds of manifestations and calls everything "the Holy Spirit."

Some of these experiences are nothing more than false antichrist spiritual manifestations which reinforce their rebellion and reward their step toward a false idea with bogus signs and wonders. Therefore, a false sense of freedom allows the Devil to keep them in bondage.

◆ Chapter Twelve

BALAAM

Balaam is a biblical name which has come to be synonymous with deception and false prophets. Balaam's name means "hardly a part of the congregation." As we take a look at this character, his name will become very apparent and highly significant in our journey towards discernment.

In the book of Revelation, Balaam is exposed by Jesus as a type of false teacher who brought false ideas into the church at Pergamos.

"But I have a few things against you, because you have there those who hold the doctrine of Balaam, who taught Balak to put a stumbling block before the children of Israel, to eat things sacrificed to idols, and to commit sexual immorality" (Revelation 2:14).

Jesus exposed this type of teaching as something which He obviously didn't appreciate in the Church. Balaam represents the results of allowing a false prophet to influence the Church.

There are two other places in the New Testament where Balaam's name is mentioned: both are references to false leadership within the Church.

Chapter Twelve

"They (false teachers) have forsaken the right way and gone astray, following the way of Balaam the son of Beor, who loved the wages of unrighteousness..." (2 Peter 2:15).

"Woe to them! For they... have run greedily in the error of Balaam for profit..." (Jude 1:11).

False prophets are just like Balaam because they love the wages of unrighteousness. Now, at first, you may assume that this only refers to the love of money; but there's a deeper meaning to this phrase, "For they have run greedily in the error of Balaam for profit..."

When you read the story of Balaam in Numbers chapters twenty-two through twenty-five, you will find that the "wages of unrighteousness" are actually called the "rewards of divination" or "diviners fee." In other words, Balaam was more interested in the rewards of divination than he was in the rewards of being a true prophet of God.

Balaam was a prophet who was hired by Balak, the evil king of the Moabites. "Balak" means "destroyer or spoiler" which, in this setting, is a parabolic picture of the Devil.

Hardly a Part of the Congregation

Since Balaam's name means "hardly a part of the congregation," it is a picture of someone who is independent and disconnected from the true Body of Christ. He represents someone who is interested in his own ministry. He is not down in the Valley of Moab camping with the rest of the children of Israel. He is off on his own prophetic campaign looking for gain and success. He loved the rewards of divination.

The story unfolds in Numbers chapter twenty-two as the Children of Israel pitch their tents on the plains of Moab. This worried the evil King Balak who immediately began to look for a way to defeat them, so the king hired Balaam to curse the Children of Israel and weaken them. He knew he couldn't fight them with natural weapons because the children of Israel were blessed by God, so the evil king turned to spiritual warfare.

The story continues as Balaam tries to do the work he was hired to do. He tries to curse the Children of Israel again and again, but he cannot succeed.

As we reach the end of the story we may even get the impression that Balaam disappeared having never fulfilled his goal. But later on, the Bible exposes Balaam as the false prophet who caused the downfall of God's people. So, how did he do it? How did he succeed in weakening the Children of Israel if it appears as if he walked away before his job was done?

The fall of the Children of Israel in the Valley of Moab is not credited to his *curses*. The emphasis is repeatedly directed towards Balaam's *teachings*. This is why Jesus exposes carnal teachings within the Church as, "the *doctrine* of Balaam" because of the power of this kind of deception (Rev. 2:14).

But if you remember the story, Balaam did not teach the children of Israel. So who did he teach?

A Dangerous Spiritual Weapon

He taught Balak. He revealed a vital, strategic plan of action that would guarantee the evil king Balak's success against the Children of Israel. Balaam gave him a spiritual key which would help destroy the people of God. By Balaam's teachings, he showed Balak (the Devil) how to cause the children of Israel to stumble and fall. The Bible clearly states that He "taught" Balak how to put a stumbling block before the children of Israel.

"The doctrine of Balaam, who taught Balak to put a stumbling block before the children of Israel, to eat things sacrificed to idols, and to commit sexual immorality" (Revelation 2:14).

Balak and Balaam could not curse these foreigners who

camped in the valley of Moab because the Children of Israel had a covenant with Almighty God. He had promised them, "I will be your shield and those who curse you will be cursed. As long as you keep My covenant, those who come against you will be defeated."

King Balak had to find a way to bypass that covenant. The only way the children of Israel could be defeated was if they forsook their covenant with God to follow other gods. This was the wonderful secret weapon that the Devil discovered through Balaam's teachings.

He Doesn't Have to Lift a Finger

The same kind of strategy is being used against the Church today. The Devil can't curse us. His spiritual warfare won't work against us. But he doesn't have to fight us because he's discovered something so powerful that it causes the Church to fall into deception and automatically activates a curse.

The Devil has learned how to put a stumbling block before God's people. The Devil doesn't have to curse the Church. All he has to do is get us to worship a wrong concept of God. A god who does not resemble Jesus Christ – a god who is quite similar to Baal or Asherah, the gods of the Moabites.

Baal and Asherah idolatry is a brilliant combination. Hand in hand, they are a powerful force.

Baal was the ultra-sovereign god of Heaven and Earth who was in complete control of all things. Depending on his mood, he could send either earthquakes or blessings. It was totally up to him. He was very hard to please and his priests enforced many strange religious requirements.

Working in covenant with Baal was Asherah. She was the goddess who promoted and approved of unbridled living. Her religion was a total commitment to satisfying the flesh. Physical or spiritual fornication were vital parts of her religious system.

In the book of Revelation, Jesus was speaking to the Christian church in Pergamos when He exposed Balaam as one who, "taught Balak to cast a stumbling-block before the children of Israel, to eat things sacrificed unto idols, and to commit fornication." It is important to note that this message is spoken to a New Testament church.

Today, the stumbling block in the Church is still the same trick that Balak used in the Old Testament: a false concept of God is placed before the people of God and they fall for it. It's an image of God which does not agree with the image of Christ. It is, essentially, the same as Baal worship.

SPIRITUAL FORNICATION

Asherah, the female goddess, also makes her way into this New Testament setting. Fornication – connected to the doctrine of Balaam – represents the "instant gratification of the flesh outside of covenant relationship."

This kind of fornication isn't physical. It is spiritual unfaithfulness. It is breaking covenant with Jesus and turning to the gratification of the flesh – in the guise of "revival."

The word, fornication, is being used here as a New Testament symbol. Esau was also mentioned in the book of Hebrews as a fornicator. "Lest there be any fornicator or profane person like Esau, who for one morsel of food sold his birthright." (Hebrews 12:16) But if you recall the story of Esau there wasn't any women involved. So why is Esau called a fornicator? Because Esau forsook his covenant blessing for a bowl of soup. He sold his future for the instant gratification of his flesh. He satisfied his belly instead of keeping his long-term relationship with God.

A portion of the Church has also forsaken its long-term covenant relationship with Jesus Christ in exchange for a wrong concept of God. A Christ-like image of God has been replaced with a god who is more like Baal and Asherah. Baal is known as the god of this world who sovereignly does whatever he pleases to his worshippers. Asherah is the god of "instant gratification of the flesh." Both of these concepts work well together and both of these concepts are pushing the true image of God out of the Church.

These new concepts of God, these new winds of doctrine, and these fresh winds of revival are presented to the Church as alternative worship to a new image of God. These options are presented to us in order to draw us away from the truth. The problem is – it's working. We are no longer covenant-keeping people. We don't even read it.

WEAKENED FROM WITHIN

We would rather have the instantaneous, the mysterious, the exciting, and the unbridled. These are the fresh spiritual manifestations of lawlessness. We have forsaken the words, "take up your cross and follow me." We no longer crucify the flesh – we caress it, entertain it, pamper it, satisfy it, and prophesy its wonderful attributes.

The Devil doesn't have to curse us. The curse is automatically activated when the Church stays in the flesh and forsakes the Word of God. The curse moves through the camp as the Devil watches from his mountain. He doesn't have to lift a finger. The Church is being weakened from within.

As the curse began to kill the children of Israel in Numbers chapter twenty five there was only one way to stop it.

"Now when Phinehas the son of Eleazar, the son of Aaron the priest, (a righteous leader) saw it (fornication) he rose from among the congregation and took a javelin in his hand; and he went after the man of Israel into the tent and thrust both of them through, the man of Israel, and the woman through her body. So the plague was stopped among the children of Israel" (Numbers 25:7-8).

There's only one way to stop the curse from going through the Church. Kill the flesh, repent, and turn back to God.

You Cannot Fix the Flesh

The Devil can't do anything to the Christian who is free from the flesh and walking in the truth. We could have such victory if we would only nail the old man to the cross with Christ.

Instead, we seek revival centers where we can counsel it, heal it, feed it, and fix it. We were never meant to walk in the flesh. It's time to crucify it. It's time to totally identify with Christ. He died to the flesh on the Cross and He wants us to follow Him. He is dead to sin and alive to God. We need to have the same commitment and attitude. This is the mind of Christ.

"Therefore, since Christ suffered for us in the flesh, arm yourselves also with the same mind, for he who has suffered in the flesh has ceased from sin, that he no longer should live the rest of his time in the flesh for the lusts of men, but for the will of God" (1 Peter 4:1-2).

The kind of teachings which satisfy and strengthen the flesh must be exposed. It's time to return to solid biblical teaching and doctrine. It's time to remember we have a new life in Christ. It's time to walk in the Spirit of truth – not in the spirit of our feelings.

If we go the way of long-term covenant relationship with Jesus and the way of the cross, then we will totally defeat the Devil. Our covenant relationship with God was meant to be based on long-term commitment and faithfulness. As long as we remain in proper relationship with God and remain grounded in His Word, then we will walk in all the benefits of covenant protection.

Chapter Twelve

"And they overcame him by the blood of the Lamb (covenant) and by the word of their testimony (the Word), and they did not love their (fleshly) lives to the death (the cross)" (Revelation 12:11).

◆ Chapter Thirteen

JANNES AND JAMBRES

Paul warned Timothy of the emptiness that was coming to the Church in the last days.

"But know this, that in the last days perilous times will come... for men will be lovers of themselves... lovers of pleasure rather than lovers of God... always learning and never able to come to the knowledge of the truth" (2 Timothy 3:1-7).

Then Paul revealed two names which expose the kind of leaders which would hold the Church captive in the last days.

"Now as Jannes and Jambres resisted Moses, so do these also resist the truth: men of corrupt minds, disapproved concerning the faith; but they will progress no further, for their folly will be manifest to all, as theirs also was" (2 Timothy 3:8-9).

Jannes means to "vex or harden" and Jambres means "foamy healer." Even as these two men resisted Moses and caused Pharaoh's heart to be hardened so it will be in the last days. These kinds of leaders will cause many to harden their hearts to the true knowledge and will of God.

God is still saying, "let my people go" but the "foamy healers" are "hardening" the hearts of the leaders and the people.

Chapter Thirteen

Why should we leave the captivity of religion and forsake all this entertainment?

The kind of teaching which comes from these "foamy healers" is nothing more than hot air dressed up as spiritual enlightenment.

Contrary to popular belief, miracles and soulish experiences do not build up believers. The real substance for faith is the Word of God – especially the Word made alive through the revelation of Christ. Miracles have never been the foundation for strong believers. The knowledge of Jesus Christ is our only true foundation. The true will of God for every believer is to become strong in the Word and to be established in biblical doctrine.

"But evil men and impostors will grow worse and worse, deceiving and being deceived. But you must continue in the things which you have learned and been assured of, knowing from whom you have learned them" (2 Timothy 3:13-14).

Just Preach the Word

Did you notice that Paul didn't instruct Timothy to battle these impostors by performing greater signs and wonders? He didn't encourage Timothy to stage a big showdown. He said, "continue in the Word Timothy, the same Holy Scriptures you've been learning since childhood. All Scripture is inspired by God and is more than enough for correction and teaching. Preach the Word, Timothy. Whether it seems convenient or not, preach the Word."

This is the only thing which is going to expose these false leaders – the solid teaching of God's Word given to committed Christians by stable leaders.

"Preach the word! Be ready in season and out of season. Convince, rebuke, exhort, with all longsuffering and teaching. For the time will come when they will not endure sound doctrine, but according to their own desires, because they have itching ears, they will heap up for themselves teachers; and they will turn their ears away from the truth, and be turned aside to fables (foolish stories)" (2 Timothy 4:2-4).

The time foretold of following fables is here. We have forsaken the Word of God as boring and mundane. We loathe this simple bread (Numbers 11:6). Yet, within it's pages is the life we're looking for. The Bible contains the bread of life from Heaven.

Jesus Christ is the true manna which rains from Heaven to strengthen His people. The true revelation and doctrine of Jesus Christ will be the powerful force which will cleanse the Church of every spot, wrinkle, and false prophet. Rest assured, the rain has already come.

We need preachers and leaders who will pick up their Bibles and learn the revelation of Christ: when they are full, they will burst forth upon the Church like huge storm clouds. Their prophetic teaching will destroy every wall that isn't founded on the Rock. The flood of God's Word will begin to wash the Church of every spot and wrinkle. Then the Church will be the glorious bride that God promised it would be.

◆ Chapter Fourteen

CLEANSING THE SPOTS AND WRINKLES

What terrifies the Devil more than anything else is the penetrating truth of God's Word reaching the hearts of men. He knows that if we settle the questions concerning the source of some of these strange manifestations, then he will be kicked out of many churches.

"That He might sanctify and cleanse her with the washing of water by the word, that He might present her to Himself a glorious Church, not having spot or wrinkle or any such thing, but that she should be holy and without blemish" (Ephesians 5:26-27).

Have you ever wondered what the spots and wrinkles are or what they represent? Many assume they are the imperfections in the life of the believer or sin in the Church. But, the Bible explains that the spots and wrinkles are more than just imperfections. The spots and wrinkles are the false leaders, false teachers, and false prophets within the Church.

"But there were also false prophets among the people, even as there will be false teachers among you..." and in verse 13 "...They are spots and blemishes, carousing in their own deceptions while they feast with you" (2 Peter 2:1).

"These (false teachers) are spots in your love feasts, while they feast with you without fear, serving only themselves..." (Jude 12).

There is a biblical way for all false prophets to be exposed and cleansed out of the Church. According to Ephesians chapter five, verses twenty-six and twenty-seven, they are going to be cleansed from the Church by the washing of the water of the Word.

Rain From Heaven

Whenever the Word of God is received as revelation or doctrine from Heaven, it is likened to rain or cleansing. The washing that Jesus is referring to is the rain of God's living Word being delivered by godly leaders who are under contract from Heaven to cleanse the Church.

The most important ingredient, which will cleanse the Church of false teachings, is the revelation of Jesus.

False prophets will not be cleansed out of the Church until believers walk in the true revelation knowledge of Christ.

Lord, Send the Rain!

Everybody wants true revival. We sing, we pray, and we preach, "Lord send the rain," without knowing what it really means. "Rain" represents something which comes from Heaven, causing vegetation and food to grow.

The "manna" came (rained) from Heaven as food for God's people.

Jesus likened Himself to manna when He said, "I am the bread from Heaven." He is the Living Word from Heaven. He said, "eat my flesh." This means that what He did and said in the flesh is food from Heaven. He came down and fed us the truth about His Father.

Chapter Fourteen

This is the true concept of revival and rain from Heaven that we should be seeking. We need to see the revelation of what Jesus showed us in His earthly ministry as the ultimate food for our spirits. There isn't a better teaching given to the Church to revive it and give it the discernment it needs.

Rain from Heaven to most people is little more than a good time at a camp-meeting. But that isn't the true meaning of rain. Revival is not a feeling.

"Ask the Lord for rain In the time of the latter rain. The Lord will make flashing clouds; He will give them showers of rain, Grass in the field for everyone" (Zechariah 10:1).

Why are we supposed to call for this kind of rain? The reason is revealed in the next verse.

"For the idols speak delusion; The diviners envision lies, And tell false dreams; They comfort in vain. Therefore the people went their way like sheep; They are in trouble because there is no shepherd" (Zechariah 10:2).

Rain is the Word from Heaven which will cleanse the Church of idols and false shepherds and provide revelation knowledge as food (grass in the field) for the strengthening of God's people (sheep) and the equipping of the Body of Christ. We desperately need the rain from Heaven to strengthen us against the false prophets and to wash their lies out of our minds.

RAIN IS A POWERFUL FORCE

Rain is not always gentle. Sometimes, rain can be a very destructive thing. The prophet Ezekiel showed us a similar concept in his prophecy in Ezekiel chapter thirteen, which reveals how God wants to destroy the walls built by false teachings with a powerful outpouring of rain.

"They have seduced my people... and one built up a wall,

and... others daubed it with untempered morter..." (Ezekiel 13:10, KJV).

Untempered mortar was the Hebrew equivalent for empty foolishness. It was a picture of someone who built a stone wall with water and sand as mortar and then covered it over with white wash. To them, there was nothing more foolish than a wall which couldn't stand up against the elements or hold back the enemy armies that often laid siege against their cities.

The false prophets were trying to build the people up with empty promises, but God told Ezekiel to prophesy against their foolishness. He called their false prophecies "untempered mortar" which was essentially building a very unstable people. God called for a mighty rain to come and destroy their foolish wall.

"They have seduced my people... and one built up a wall, and... others daubed it with untempered morter... it shall fall: there shall be an overflowing shower; and ye, O great hailstones, shall fall; and a stormy wind shall rend it... there shall be an overflowing shower... So will I break down the wall that ye have daubed with untempered morter (foolish teachings and prophecies), and bring it down to the ground, so that the foundation thereof shall be discovered (exposed), and it shall fall... and ye shall know that I am the LORD" (Ezekiel 13:10-14, KJV).

True Revival Will Not Fall Into Our Laps

God is prophetically promising the New Testament Church that the Living Word of God was going to come from Heaven as a great rain and outpouring in the form of revelation and solid teaching to rid the Church of false teaching and false prophets.

We will not find a passive way to accomplish this task. Revival will not fall into our laps. Furthermore, this kind of revival is not found in Toronto, Ontario or Pensacola, Florida. It

Chapter Fourteen

can only come through strong leaders giving solid teaching to committed believers.

With hypnotic repetition, we've heard the phrase, "It is time to put our doctrines aside." But I say, "No! Do not listen to such disarming statements. Do not put your doctrines aside!" It's as if "doctrine" has become a dirty word in the Church. More than ever, it's time to concentrate on our doctrine. We must expose the false unstable concepts of God that are imbedded and hidden within our teachings and our traditions. It is time to replace them with the solid teachings of the Living Word.

The Devil would just love it if we remained little, ignorant, childish Christians tossed to and fro by every new wind of teaching. He would be pleased with us if we remained easy to push around like empty little clouds with no content.

A wind of teaching comes along and "poof," off we go. There's no stability in the Church because there's no stability in our doctrines. We've become as empty as the false prophets we follow.

Empty Nonsense

Jude 12 says of false teachers, "clouds they are without water, carried about of winds; trees whose fruit withereth, without fruit..." (KJV).

2 Peter 2:17 calls them "wells without water, clouds carried by a tempest."

These are leaders who are filled with nothing but a bunch of empty nonsense. The Church is being taken in by an abundance of flesh and empty words.

"Let no one deceive you with empty words..." (Ephesians 5:6).

"They speak great swelling words of emptiness... (vanity, foolishness)" (2 Peter 2:18).

No longer should we be tossed to and fro like empty little clouds. We should be more like huge prophetic thunder clouds filled with the water of the Word. Clouds are supposed to carry valuable rain, not useless vapor. The latter rain from Heaven is ultimately the Word of God made alive through Jesus. A true latter days prophet or leader will reveal the whole counsel of God through the fullness of Jesus and expose the emptiness of antichrist teachings.

The only way to deal with emptiness is to get full. It's time to get into our Bibles and learn. We are being deceived because we are following the latest fluff instead of grounding ourselves in the Word.

When we get to the place where we desire the richness of the Word of God more than satisfying our flesh at some crazy out-of-control-camp-meeting, then we will be able to truly discern today's remaining flakey preachers.

Lord, send the rain!

◆ Testing the Spirits Resources

BOOKS:

Men Who Devour Men: *Wolves Among Us*

BOOKLETS

God Does Make Sense

Jesus Christ – Solid Rock: *Re-establishing the Church on its Original Foundation*

VIDEOS

Thorns and Thistles: *Fresh insight into the meaning of Paul's thorn in the flesh*

Is There Life After Charismania? *April, 1998, Discernment Seminar in Edmonton, Alberta*

The Parable Behind Speaking in Tongues: *A video series featuring a re-evaluation of tongues*

AUDIOS

I Was A Flakey Preacher: *Conference series recorded at Toronto's Discernment Ministries Canada Conference November 1997*

FREE NEWSLETTER

To receive our free newsletter dealing with contemporary Christian issues, send your mailing address to;

Testing The Spirits, 9739-99 St. Westlock, Alberta, T7P 1Y5

For copies of this book,
other teaching materials, catalogs,
audios, videos, or a free newsletter

please contact:

Ted Brooks
Testing the Spirits
9739-99 St.
Westlock, Alberta, Canada
T7P 1Y5

Phone: 780-349-8209
Toll free for orders: 800-816-TEST (8378)

Watch for our new Web Site
Early Spring 1999
WWW.TESTINGTHESPIRITS.COM
Internet's Premier Christian Discernment Site